SCARBOROUGH

Produced in cooperation with the
Scarborough Chamber of Commerce

Windsor Publications, Ltd.
Burlington, Ontario

SCARBOROUGH

Windsor Publications, Inc.—History Books Division
Managing Editor: Karen Story
Design Director: Alexander d'Anca

Staff for *Scarborough: An Economic Celebration*
Manuscript Editor: Karl Stull
Associate Editor: Jeffrey Reeves
Photo Editor: Laura Cordova
Senior Production Editor, Corporate Profiles: Phyllis Gray
Editor, Corporate Profiles: Brenda Berryhill
Senior Proofreader: Susan J. Muhler
Editorial assistants: Didier Beauvoir, Thelma Fleischer, Kim Kievman, Rebecca Kropp,
   Michael Nugwynne, Kathy B. Peyser, Pat Pittman, Theresa J. Solis
Publisher's Representative, Corporate Profiles: Ray Payne, Irene Vogan
Layout Artist, Corporate Profiles: Bonnie Felt
Designer: Bradford Boston
Layout Artist: Christina L. Rosepapa

Windsor Publications, Ltd.
Elliot Martin, Chairman of the Board
James L. Fish III, Chief Operating Officer

*Previous page: The Toronto Hunt
Club overlooks the Scarborough
Bluffs. Courtesy, City of Scarborough*

*Facing page: The sun shines
through the trees at Milliken Park.
Photo by Glen Jones*

This book is dedicated to the people of the City of Scarborough
by the Scarborough Chamber of Commerce

CONTENTS

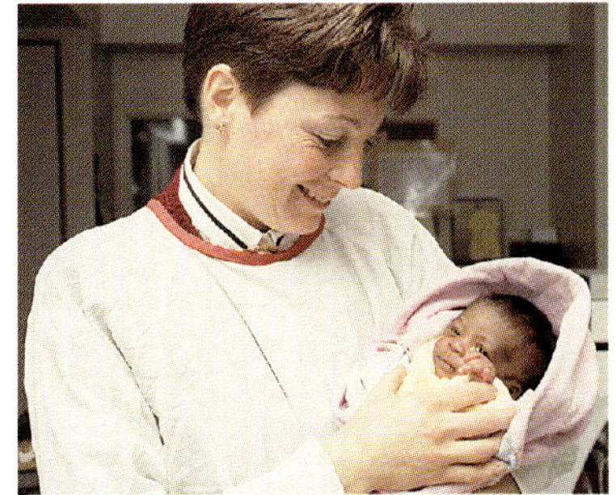

Photo by Glen Jones

Photo by Glen Jones

PART ONE

A SPECIAL CITY

CHAPTER ONE

The Making of a Special City

In the summer of 1987, a man named Clark Secor passed away at the advanced age of 98. He had been known for many years as "Mr. Scarborough," having been honoured by the Scarborough City Council in 1979, on his 90th birthday, as the city's "longest-living son."

Secor was a crusty fellow in his later years, with a long life that stretched from Scarborough's rural last century all the way to its incarnation as a world-class city in the late 1980s. In fact, he was the great-grandson of the township's first reeve, and was born and raised on his father's farm in what is today's Agincourt area, just north of the bustling Civic Centre. He spent hundreds of hours in his later years sharing his warm memories with the youth of the city.

"Secor loved speaking to children and telling them how things were, before Scarborough was a city," says a friend. "He would tell them about life on the farm and about going into Toronto to get supplies for his father's store. The kids would send him all kinds of letters saying how much they enjoyed his talks."

Secor is greatly missed, and he was much loved over his nearly 10 full decades in Scarborough. His life neatly frames the quite remarkable metamorphosis of his native city, and serves as a good introduction to this dynamic community.

Scarborough, Ontario—one of the largest cities in Canada—lies on the eastern edge of the Metropolitan Toronto area, which has a total population of over 3.2 million people. Scarborough has usually been overshadowed by its more famous older sibling to its southwest, even though it shares many municipal services with the city of Toronto, as well as North York, York, East York, and Etobicoke. Indeed, they are all part of the quite inspired metropolitan system of government—the first in the world of its kind.

Because of its late blossoming, and still later debut as an actual city, Scarborough was, for many decades, seen as a kind of dull bedroom community for Toronto, a place where one could get an inexpensive "starter" home for half the price of mid-town Toronto, just a few minutes' drive to the west, perhaps even less. It was the area where thousands of new immigrants would flock—hoping to build a new life in a strange land. It was seen as strongly working-class—as if there is anything wrong with that.

Scarborough was considered the ugly duckling, a minor suburb of the real city. And for many years it was, with its thousands of little brick homes, and its long, broad streets filled with car dealerships and fast-food outlets.

But ugly ducklings often turn out to be swans, as every child knows. And many a suburb can become a super-city, almost overnight. That's precisely what happened to the city of Scarborough.

What is surprising, perhaps, is that it took as long as it did. After all, more than any other borough or city within 300 kilometres in any direction, it had magnificent natural beauty. The famed Scarborough Bluffs stretch 15 kilometres along its shoreline, and rise up to 64 metres above Lake Ontario. It has a superb location; superior transportation and communications networks; generous available space; a mas-

The sun reflects off one of the Consilium Place buildings. Photo by Lorraine C. Parrow/ First Light

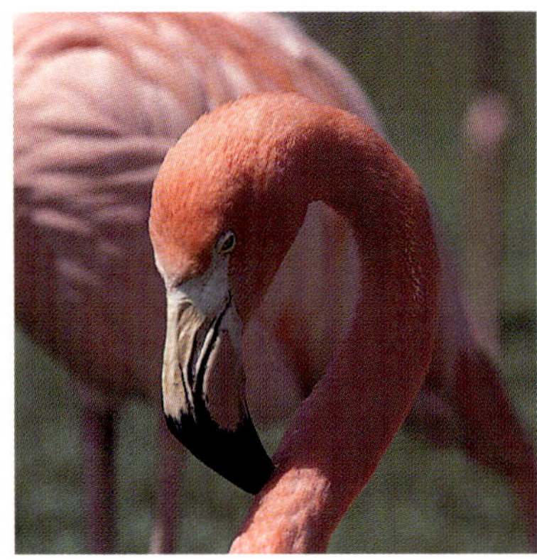

Above: These flamingos can be found at the Toronto Zoo. Photo by Lorraine C. Parrow/First Light

Below: An inviting pathway leads pedestrians through Scarborough Bluffs Park. Photo by Glen Jones

sive, highly skilled labour pool; a generous 5,000 acres of parkland; excellent hospitals; one of the best zoos in the world; and, thanks to a fine public school system, a top-notch university and college. Scarborough has achieved a quality of life that would be hard to match in all of North America.

Granted, the climate of Scarborough is hardly that of San Diego or the Caribbean, although most visitors are surprised to hear that the city lies on about the same latitude as Rome, Italy. The terrain of the entire Metro Toronto area also leaves much to be desired, lacking the great mountainous beauty of Montreal to the east, or Vancouver to the west. That's why Scarborough's generous amount of exquisite parkland is all the more precious.

And while many of those "little boxes" remain in Scarborough, the bustling city also has its luxurious homes and mansions as well, with winding roads and exclusive neighbourhoods, just like any other fine community. Thanks to the inspired city fathers and mothers, there are also a number of gorgeous buildings, many of them built over the past decade or two, such as the Civic Centre, the new Consilium, and more.

Scarborough grew up where it did because it was near Lake Ontario, and on the edge of the capital city of the province of Ontario. Yet Scarborough remained primarily rural and farmland, right into this century. The close to half a million residents of the late 1980s probably are unaware that fewer than 4,000 people lived in the township of Scarborough just nine decades ago. Only a few thousand—but they were sagacious souls.

One of the keys to Scarborough's recent successes has clearly been the hundreds of companies that have wisely chosen to build there, including Alcan Aluminum, Bick's, Burroughs Office Supplies, Dad's Cookies, Royal Doulton Canada, Ecko, Fibreglass Canada, Ford Glass,

*Above: St. Peter and Paul Ukran-
ian Catholic Church reflects the diversity of Scarborough's ethnicity.
Photo by Glen Jones*

*Left: The Guild Inn welcomes visit-
ors and guests as well as local artists. Photo by Glen Jones*

*Below: Scarborough offers a range
of lifestyles in a city of varied neigh-
borhoods. Courtesy, City of Scarborough*

General Motors, Honda, Honeywell, Laura Secord, McGraw-Hill, Na-
bisco, Noma, Pascal Furniture, Prudential, SKF, State Farm Insurance, Ther-
mos, Toyota, Volkswagen, and Warner-Lambert. There are hundreds
of others, too, attracted by quality of services, good housing, and a welcoming municipal government.

But in the final analysis, a city is its people. And people demand a
good life for themselves and their families, or they won't come and
they won't stay. Scarborough has been offering a good life for several decades now—even though it has taken its neighbours a long time to
realize that fact. Indeed, Chinese, Japanese, and Swedish firms discovered the excellence of Scarborough many years before its fellow cities
in Metropolitan Toronto ever did.

Myths die hard, and it won't be overnight that Scarborough is
finally recognized as the striving, thriving city that it has become.

CHAPTER TWO

A Look at Our History

n the mid-1950s, a steam-shovel operator working in the heart of today's Scarborough—Bellamy Road north of Lawrence Avenue, to be exact—tore open an ancient Indian burial pit full of bones. Ethnologists soon pounced on the scene, and began to piece together the remarkable Iroquois culture that existed over seven centuries ago, exactly where over half a million Scarborough residents now live, work, and thrive.

The history of modern Scarborough is not much older than the Second World War. But those ancient Indian bones may help us to recognize that even in the twelfth century, groups of native Canadians also recognized the area was a good place to raise their families.

The true origins of the booming Scarborough of today don't go back much farther than two centuries ago, yet the city has its own healthy collection of published histories. One was printed in 1896, on Scarborough's 100th anniversary, and a handsome brochure was put out in 1959 to celebrate a visit by Queen Elizabeth. But the definitive one is surely *A History of Scarborough*, edited by the Reverend Robert R. Bonis and published by the city's public library in 1968. It is from that volume that this writer gratefully draws the following facts, with all due thanks and credit to the Reverend Bonis.

It's been only 350 years since French fur traders paddled by Scarborough's great cliffs in canoes, and less than 200 years since the first surveyor of the tiny township translated what the explorers had labelled the stunning bluffs, "Les Grandes Ecores," into English, "The High Lands of Toronto."

Iroquois Indians were probably farming in Scarborough as early as 900 years ago, about the time of William the Conqueror. The radio-carbon dating of remains from their village placed it in the twelfth century, when its inhabitants lived mainly by raising crops and fishing. The fishing is still excellent off the bluffs, and backyard gardens are still popular, but land has become too expensive for major farming anymore, at least within the city limits.

The Indians who dwelt in Scarborough lived in five large multiple-family longhouses, and fortified their village well, suggesting that they had enemies. Indeed, skeletons were found that had arrow points lodged in their spines.

The white, English-speaking history of Scarborough begins about two centuries ago—August 4, 1793, to be exact—when Elizabeth Simcoe, the wife of Lieutenant Governor John Graves Simcoe, made the first recorded, and favourable, comment in her diary upon the beautiful scenery—and gave the future city its name at the same time:

We came within sight of what is named in the Map the high lands of Toronto—the shore is extremely bold and has the appearance of Chalk Cliffs . . . They appeared so well that we talked of building a Summer Residence there and calling it Scarborough.

The initial surveyor of the township east of Toronto, one Augustus Jones, had been told to lay out an area known as "Glasgow," back in

This illustration showing the Iroquoian Feast of the Dead, is from Claude LeBeau's Avantures du Sr. C. Le Beau, *Amsterdam, 1738. Courtesy, Metropolitan Toronto*

Above: The magnificent Scarborough Bluffs are reflected in the still waters of Lake Ontario. Photo by Glen Jones

Right: The Rouge River swells with melting snow each spring. Photo by Glen Jones

1791, but that name was soon discarded. Elizabeth Simcoe had recognized the similarity between these great gray cliffs and those she had seen back in the English Yorkshire town, and her name for the area was the one that stuck.

The growth would be slow over the next century. Governor Simcoe offered generous grants of land in those closing years of the eighteenth century, and a number of pioneers began to move into the area. There are dozens of rather charming stories, but let just one—the earliest—suffice, for it underlines just how recently Canada has gone from primitive settlements to the electronic age.

The same year Elizabeth Simcoe christened this city, a gentleman named Charles Annis came up to Canada from the recently founded United States of America with his wife, children, oxen, mare, colt, and heifer. He was offered a 100-acre lot in what is today downtown Toronto, where the Eaton Centre now stands, in exchange for his two-year-old heifer. For some reason, he wasn't particularly impressed with what was then the fledgling town of York, and chose to proceed

Left: This historic scene depicts an important moment in Iroquois history - the pulling together of warring tribes to mold together the oldest form of government, the Five Nations. Courtesy, Onondaga County Savings Bank

Below left: John Graves Simcoe, right, is shown in this 1773 William Pars painting with John Burridge Cholwick, seated, and Archdeacon Andrew, left. Courtesy, Metropolitan Toronto Library

Below: Elizabeth Postuma Simcoe, wife of John Graves Simcoe, documented her travels into the interior with her husband with drawings and observations. Courtesy, Metropolitan Toronto Library

eastward, through the heavily timbered wilderness, to the heights of present-day Scarborough. He had passed up one of the biggest real estate coups since the Indians sold Manhattan Island for a few dollars in jewelry, all for an unknown future to the east. It would be over a century and a half before history would prove Charles Annis correct in placing his faith in Scarborough.

The young farmer camped for a while at what is today Kingston Road and Eglinton Avenue, surrounded by maple, beech, and pine trees, moved on a bit further east, and left his two oldest boys to chop down some of those handsome trees and establish squatter's rights to the then unsurveyed land.

By 1808, Annis returned to live on a farm in today's Scarborough, where his son and daughter-in-law, Levi and Rhoda, kept a public house which was popular for many years. The liquor laws of Ontario were considerably more lenient back then. In this old inn, the son and daughter-in-law of our pioneering hero raised a dozen children. Not all of them made it to adulthood, as can be seen on the tombstones in the tiny cemetery behind the present Washington United Church at Kingston Road and Eglinton Avenue.

Many years later, a solid stone house was built by the Annis' 11th child, Jeremiah. It was 1867, the year that Canada became a dominion. The house still stands, not far from the site of the old inn of that family, on the north side of Kingston Road, opposite the church.

So it went, throughout the nineteenth century, although quite slowly at first. Some of the names of these pioneering men and women are lost, but many others live on, honoured in the parks and streets of today's Scarborough, including David Thomson, for instance. He was a Scottish stone mason who came to the New World to erect new government buildings in York. He took an axe and headed for the banks of Highland Creek, not far from the site of the present Scarborough General Hospital, and built a healthful home for his wife and children, far from the marshes near Toronto bay, which were known to cause fever and ague. Thomson soon owned 600 acres of some of the finest land in Upper Canada, and by 1799 was granted 200 more acres, thanks to

This Morrish Store looks virtually unchanged from when it was built in 1890. Photo by Glen Jones

his petition claiming himself as "the first settler who had built a house and resided in Scarborough."

In 1802, a half-dozen years after the first permanent settlement of Scarborough, there were but 89 inhabitants. Of the township's 45,000 acres, only 170 were assessed as cultivated land. In the census of 1809, only 34 men, 24 women, and 82 children under the age of 16 lived in the entire vast township. Thousands of acres were held by speculators who were unwilling to rough it in the bush, and over one-third of the area belonged to the crown and clergy, which was a pattern throughout Ontario.

War would also have an effect on migration—in Scarborough's case, lessening it. After the War of 1812 between England and the United States, Britain was wary about some of the revolutionary qualities of the Yankees affecting its dominion, so they decided to put a stop to all further American immigration. The result can be captured in a simple statistic: as late as 1819—over a quarter-century after the first settlers came to Scarborough—the community numbered less than 350 people. Obviously, the great potential of the area remained untapped for some time.

But the great nineteenth-century movement of men and women from Great Britain to the New World accelerated after the first few decades of the last century. The 477 inhabitants of Scarborough in 1820 more than doubled to 1,135 in 1830, and by 1845, over 650 families were farming in the little boomtown.

By mid-century, the pioneering years appeared to be over, as nearly 4,000 souls hacked it out near the beautiful Scarborough Bluffs. Three gristmills were already working away, as were nearly two dozen sawmills, feeding the thriving ship-building industry. As early as 1839, a total of 18 miles of Kingston Road was already paved with planks, over which farmers were daily hauling lumber, cordwood, grain, and potatoes past toll gates on the way to the burgeoning city of Toronto, which had changed its name from York just two years before. There are tolls no longer between Scarborough and Toronto, which proves that some things, at least, get cheaper over the years.

Scarborough village had its own post office as early as 1832, but it would not become a true rural township until the last half of the nineteenth century. It was in 1850 that Scarborough was formally incorporated as a municipality, with its first Township Council meeting held in a tavern at Markham and Old Danforth. One should not assume that this choice of meeting place was by chance; as early as 1834, the minister of St. Andrew's Church felt it necessary to organize a temperance society, and a division of the Sons of Temperance was organized in Scarborough in 1855.

In 1877, just over 11 decades ago, the provincial secretary for Scarborough reported that $5,602 was raised in taxes to support the township's 11 schools. When one considers that a beginning teacher in Scarborough's schools in this decade begins his/her career at close to $25,000 a year, one can see just how little the 1877 levy would cover today.

In that same year, $3,490 was spent on roads and bridges, an amount which might barely cover a few coffee breaks for a 1980s work crew on Sheppard Avenue East.

There was even a Scarborough Library from the township's very beginnings, although for its first 44 years, it depended for support on a membership of less than four dozen. By 1878, it had some 1,100 volumes, and with a special government grant of $400 the next year, it broadened its collection considerably. One could purchase quite a few books for $400 in those days.

The year 1896 marked Scarborough's centenary, and there were some flashy celebrations at St. Andrew's Church that June, with lots

Rouge Beach Park is a haven for all kinds of wildlife, including this swan enjoying the calm waters. Photo by Glen Jones

Above: St. Andrews was built in 1849, and was the site of centennial celebrations in 1896. Photo by Glen Jones

Below: St. Margaret's Anglican Church retains the charm of a country church. Photo by Glen Jones

of presumably tedious addresses by such people as the lieutenant governor, leisurely performances by the festival choir, bands, and bagpipers, and the singing of "The Maple Leaf Forever," the very patriotic and exceedingly popular song written by none other than Scarborough's own Alexander Muir, who was a schoolteacher.

These were clearly growth years. In 1880, the Ontario Agricultural Commission reported that over 33,000 acres, or over three-quarters the land of Scarborough, was cleared of trees. The same civil servants also discovered that an acre was going for between $80 and $110. But before one gets too depressed, recall that $100 was almost a full year's salary for most people in North America, just a century ago.

There wasn't much need for a chamber of commerce back then, but capitalism was certainly rearing its vibrant head. By 1896, there were 10 dairies in Scarborough, helping to produce milk, butter, and cheese for the tens of thousands of people in the metropolitan area to the southwest.

Indeed, the draw of the neighbouring city of Toronto was a strong one. While Toronto grew from 86,000 souls in 1881 to over 180,000 ten years later, the population of rural Scarborough actually declined from a modest peak of 4,615 in 1871 to a mere 3,711 in 1900. The reasons were many, but here's a simple one: the 23 sawmills which boomed in the township in the 1850s and 1860s closed down one by one as the last century progressed and the supply of timber was continually depleted.

Scarborough, so exciting and burgeoning in the past few decades, was really only a gathering of farms and villages well into this century. In fact, its population declined to a modern low of 3,426 in 1910, before more than tripling, to 11,746, shortly after the end of World War I.

It was only in the teens of the present century, to quote historian Bonis, that Scarborough "began to turn its back upon its rural past and . . . look forward to its suburban, residential and industrial future."

Transportation grew in importance. The late 1890s found hundreds of cyclists biking back and forth between Scarborough and neighbouring townships and cities. In 1898, the Toronto Railway Company laid its first rails along Kingston Road—an impressive feat, but still a far cry from the city's remarkable rapid transit system of the 1980s.

Hundreds of Torontonians began to build summer cottages along the magnificent bluffs, and pressing new demands came for roads, schools, sidewalks, streetlights, water mains, hydro-electric power, and all those things we take so much for granted today.

Little wood-frame churches popped up, although some congregations could only dig basements and wait anxiously for a growing population to help pay for the building to rise above it. That would come. By 1925, over 15,000 called Scarborough home; by the end of World War II, over 25,000.

Then Scarborough really exploded. With the end of World War II came tens of thousands of servicemen, along with masses of valued immigrants to this country. Their need for homes, schools, and businesses would mark the true beginning of the modern city of Scarborough.

In the mid-1940s, and right through the next two decades, farm after farm was gobbled up by bulldozers, with the occasional Indian burial ground dug up along the way. New housing subdivisions sprouted as rapidly as fields of grain had sprouted in the exact same places during the previous two centuries. Apartment buildings shot up, as did large factories and industrial parks. The 25,000 residents of what was little more than a bedroom community of Toronto turned it into the fastest growing community in all of Canada.

By 1950, the township nearly doubled in numbers, to over 48,000.

By 1955, it was over 110,000; by 1960, nearly 200,000. Scarborough became a textbook case of postwar building and population boom.

Seemingly overnight, the farmlands along Eglinton Avenue, running east from Victoria Park, were transformed into the impressive business and industrial complex known as the Golden Mile. Modern plants appeared as if by magic, right across the then borough of Scarborough. The sleepy farming community which had only recently boasted of grist- and sawmills, as well as dairies, now began to turn out automotive parts, long-playing records, typewriters, refrigerators, glass, plastic, paper, candy, cosmetics, household electrical items, and a thousand other consumer products.

By 1960, over 500 industries—not businesses, but actual industries—had been established in Scarborough. And with the coming of the majestic Highway 401, which sweeps from Windsor/Detroit on the southwest to Montreal on the northeast, the boom could only continue. Shopping plazas also sprang up across the community, beginning with the famous Eglinton Square Shopping Centre, which was the first to appear, at the end of the Golden Mile.

The growth of Scarborough was also assisted by the creation of the Municipality of Metropolitan Toronto by an act of the Ontario provincial government on January 1, 1954. This bill did nothing less than unite Scarborough with a dozen other towns and boroughs in the area under a common government. This relieved the booming township of such responsibilities as its waterworks, sewage disposal, police, capital expenditures for schools, arterial roads, and other costly matters.

The township of Scarborough showed an even greater sensitivity to the leisure needs of its growing populace than it did its commercial requirements. Even before the First World War, Scarborough began to acquire parkland. It started with less than a dozen acres of Scarborough Bluffs in 1911, and continued to acquire land over the years, especially during the postwar boom. By as early as 1963, the Recreation and Parks Commission held and maintained for its citizens nearly 100 parks, parkettes, playgrounds, woods, and ravines.

As of the late 1980s, there are discussions, even arguments, over how much of the remaining parkland should be saved in Scarborough, and whether much-needed, even demanded, housing should be allowed to encroach upon the wilderness. But these are questions every major city must face, and as Scarborough moves toward the twenty-first century, it will have to confront many such tough challenges. If the past is any judge, it will handle them with intelligence.

To move from Scarborough's early Indian inhabitants to the Nuclear Age took hundreds of years, yet in this chapter it was achieved in but a few pages. What is more extraordinary, however, is the way the township/borough/city of Scarborough managed to go from a few dozen hardy pioneers to a few thousand suburbanites to nearly half a million working, playing, studying, travelling, earning, spending, thinking, feeling, thriving city-dwellers, all in less than two centuries, a mere blink of the eye of history.

Scarborough has been a city since 1983, but had the potential of a supercity since Charles Annis refused to give up his heifer for land in downtown Toronto, and chose to move with his family to the golden east. Certainly, the Annis clan knew what they were doing.

Since the Second World War, so have hundreds of thousands of other men, women, and children, who have made Scarborough their home, their place of business, and their place of leisure. Scarborough, certainly over the last few decades, has proven itself to be no mean city.

This is the grand entrance to 100 & 200 Consilium Place. Photo by Glen Jones

CHAPTER THREE

Parks, Sports, and Other Fun

With the most parkland in all of Metropolitan Toronto, as well as the magnificent Scarborough Bluffs, sweeping down to wonderful beaches, marinas, and fishing, the city of Scarborough is one of the best in North America for recreation.

How did this young community manage to preserve so much parkland? That decision can be traced back to before World War I, when the rural area began to be invaded by suburban subdivisions from the nearby metropolis of Toronto. The township responded, with great inspiration, by acquiring parklands, beginning with 10 acres of Scarborough Bluffs Park and the 2.5-hectare Tott's Park, also on the bluffs, in 1911.

Then, as the building boom in Scarborough really took off, the Township Council realized that it needed a clearly defined policy to provide parks for the swelling population. From 1950 to the present, the new Recreation and Parks Commission proceeded to develop and add to its holdings, year after year. By 1963, the commission both held and maintained for the citizens of Scarborough some 98 parks, parkettes, playfields, playgrounds, woods, and ravines, comprising a total of nearly 324 hectares.

Yet Scarborough has never been one to rest on its already substantial, God-given laurels. The men and women who have lived and worked in the city over the past century created services, clubs, sporting events, and more, making Scarborough a haven for sports enthusiasts.

To list everything the city of Scarborough offers would take another book the size of this one. So here is just a brief selection of the recreation this extraordinary city provides.

Scarborough has nearly 800 hectares of parks today, filled with everything from picnicking areas to interesting sights. The largest of these are the so-called district parks, including Thomson Park, Cedar Brook Park, L'Amoreaux Park, and Milliken Park. Many of these offer marvelous outdoor winter activities, such as cross-country skiing, ice skating, and hair-raising tobogganing.

A number of the over 200 parks in the city actually remain forested, something not frequently found in most North American cities. Some even have natural trails through them, along which one can observe a great variety of birds and wildlife, as well as often rare and unusual species of trees, plants, and wildflowers.

There are parks which have formal gardens, such as the aforementioned Thomson Park, and the Cedar Ridge Creative Centre. The Scarborough Historical Museum is located within Thomson Park, on Brimley Road, just north of Lawrence Avenue East. The museum includes Cornell House, which depicts a rural village family home from about the turn of the century, when Scarborough was not much more than a collection of farms. Also found there is the McCowan Log Cabin, which allows adults and children to see how early settlers lived during the midnineteenth century. The Hough Carriage Works, also on the grounds, displays tools used by a local Scarborough carriage maker, whose

Four marinas give sailors ample opportunity to enjoy sailing and fishing along the bluffs. Courtesy, City of Scarborough

Right: L'Amoreaux Park is one of the "district parks" in Scarborough. Courtesy, City of Scarborough

Below: Scarborough enjoys more parkland than any other city in Metro Toronto. Courtesy, City of Scarborough

A variety of trees characterize Milliken Park. Photo by Glen Jones

Right: Mist rises on a peaceful morning along the Scarborough Nature Trail. Photo by Glen Jones

Below right: In some of Scarborough's natural trails, a variety of birds and wildlife can be observed. Photo by Glen Jones

Above: The Cedar Ridge Arts and Craft Centre is surrounded by colourful flowers. Photo by Glen Jones

Above right: It's hard to choose from the array of activities posted outside the Cornell House Museum. Photo by Glen Jones

Below: Authentic tools and supplies bring the past alive at Hough Carriage Works. Photo by Jack Holman

descendants probably work at GM, Toyota, or Honda.

There is also a good selection of glorious waterfront parks within the city of Scarborough, which are operated by the Metro Parks and Property Department. They range from East Point Park, where cars are not allowed, but where one can walk along the top of the bluffs and follow trails down to the shore, to Rouge Beach Park, which has a superb sand beach, change rooms, and a canoe club.

Other waterfront parks include Guildwood Park, which surrounds the lovely Guild Inn, Cathedral Bluffs, Cudia Park, and Bluffers Park. The latter offers one of the few opportunities to reach the water's edge by automobile and to view the beauty of the bluffs from a lower vantage point.

In many marinas, the public is fenced out. But not so at the very beautiful Bluffers Park marina, where the non-boating public can hang around with the sailors and have a meal or a drink at the public restaurant. People can walk along the docks close to the boats. Soon there will be more boats than ever, as the new marina doubles the 500 moorings there.

There are, today, an unbelievable total of four successful yacht clubs in Scarborough, including Cathedral Bluffs, Bluffers Park, Highland, and Scarborough Bluffs, each developed and built by its members.

The Cathedral Bluffs Yacht Club was the first one to form, back in 1977, with an original "dirty 30" members, who built up membership to over 260 boats by 1987. Scarborough Bluffs Yacht Club is the only one that's a "dry sailor," which means that it brings its boats out of the water after each use. The Bluffers Park Boating Federation built its docks, did the landscaping, and financed its club houses on the reclaimed land developed by the Metro Parks.

The four clubs are active in racing with one another, and they all have good relations with each other, reciprocally providing free services for one another.

Other attractions abound onshore. The two 18-hole Metro golf courses within the boundaries of Scarborough, Dentonia Park and Tam O'Shanter, are both rated moderately difficult, while the horseback

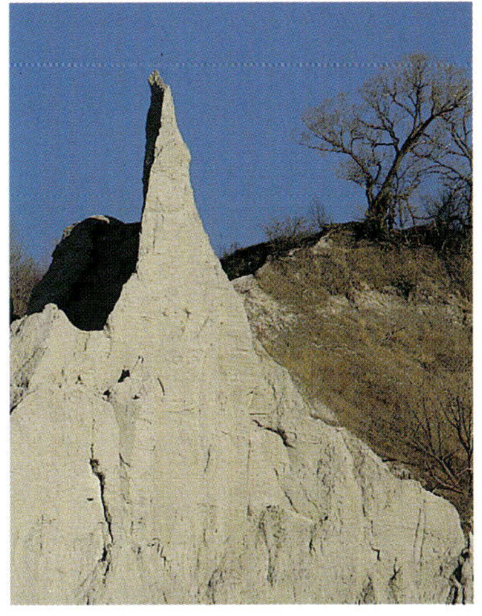

Above: Cathedral Bluffs, one of Scarborough's glorious waterfront parks, is operated by the Metro Parks and Property Department. Photo by Glen Jones

Below: The Guild Inn Gardens feature breathtaking sculpture amid the flowers and fountains. Photo by Dawn Goss/First Light

Dramatic bluffs meet Lake Ontario at Scarborough Bluffs Park.
Photo by Glen Jones

riding, offered at Rouge Hills Stables, is as challenging or gentle as you choose. And the bicycle paths, in four different areas of the city, meander along streams and through ravine parks overflowing with woods and open meadows, not to mention the jogging routes, with specially-designed exercise stations.

Since 1986, Neighbourhood Walks have been mapped out along public sidewalks, through local parks, and along several hydro corridors in the northwest corner of the city. Signs offer simple directions to the hundreds who have taken advantage of these delightful walks, and explanatory leaflets are available at the Civic Centre. It is just one more example of Scarborough's charm, and one more reason why more and more of its residents have become active and in love with its very big outdoors.

Three times a year, the city of Scarborough sends a brochure to the over 160,000 households across its vast municipal area. It overflows with listings of classes in aquatics, music, art, dance, skating, gymnastics, and soccer for everyone from preschoolers to school-age children, teens, and adults. Older residents have such additional options as arts and crafts, table tennis, martial arts, skiing, skating, hockey, badminton, basketball, floor hockey, bowling, volleyball, wrestling, fencing, golf, netball, tennis, and even a rifle club.

Older citizens benefit from services ranging from community clubs to drop-in centres, and from arts and crafts to dance, educational programmes, and even indoor golf practice.

The disabled are not overlooked. Developmentally handicapped children enjoy summer day camps, as do physically disabled children and teens. There is even a day camp for children with learning disabilities.

There are winter programmes, as well, for physically and mentally disabled children. Therapy pool programmes. Recreation clubs. Bowling and hockey teams for the disabled. A hockey club and bowling league for the visually impaired. A swim club for children and teens with mental disabilities. A weekly social programme for individuals who have suffered strokes. A recreation club for the hearing-impaired.

This golfer takes careful aim at the Scarborough Golf Club. Photo by Jack Holman

One could go on and on, for there are many more such offerings. For the one in seven in Metro Toronto who have some kind of physical or mental disability, the city of Scarborough is a very good place to live.

The city of Scarborough used to run a dashing photo of angler Kurt Hilgendorf proudly clutching a 25-pound trophy rainbow trout. Unbelievable as it seems, the IBM employee caught the fish in Lake Ontario, just off Scarborough's Bluffers Park.

For reasons best known to Mother Nature, the Ice Age created a unique underwater environment at the foot of those majestic bluffs. One can catch, with little difficulty and time, salmon which range in weight from 25 to 35 pounds, and a wide selection of rainbows, lakers, and browns in the 6- to 20-pound range.

Of course, there is one catch (pun intended): this pleasure is only allowed during the six-month trophy fishing season.

Now, how many world-class cities have world-class fishing just a few kilometres south of their downtown?

Scarborough also hosts the dynamic and impressive Peace Games. For over 15 years the people of Indianapolis, Indiana, and Scarborough have competed in athletics. Established in 1973, the Peace Games evolved into a mini-Olympiad, featuring many different sports and competitors who range in age from 10 to 65.

The Indianapolis-Scarborough Peace Games are held in August and rotate annually between the two cities. But these are more than just competitions. Their importance, and their popularity, lies in their sheer neighbourliness. All competitors, coaches, managers, and executives stay with their counterparts in the host city. This has led to cultural exchange and countless, long-lasting friendships between the residents of the cities, which are a 10-hour, 340-kilometre trip apart.

But the distance vanishes every summer, as over 1,700 people compete, and hundreds more share in the organization and billeting of the visiting athletes each year. It's a simply inspired idea, and at its heart is the quotation which the Peace Games uses on its brochure: "In an age where winning is everything, it is encouraging to witness an event that teaches athletes to first become good sports!"

From bowling to arm-wrestling, from badminton to basketball, from ping-pong to horseshoes, the Peace Games is one more reason why Scarborough is so lively, and so liveable.

Another reason is the Robbie International Soccer Tournament, which for more than two decades has turned Scarborough into nothing less than the North American capital of youth soccer. It began, back in 1967, with two purposes: to gain recognition for youth soccer, and to raise funds to battle cystic fibrosis. Robbie Wimbs, the tournament's namesake, has the disease, and inspired the concept.

When that first tiny handful of teams took the field, no one could have imagined what the tournament would become. By the late 1980s, the Robbie attracted over 8,000 players of both sexes, all ages and many nationalities. Scarborough hosted teams from across the United States, Holland, West Germany, Egypt, and Nigeria. And the Robbie soon began to collect money to fight muscular dystrophy as well as cystic fibrosis.

Over the years, many hundreds of thousands of dollars have been raised by volunteer clubs for the two diseases, and Robbie Wimbs is today in his late 20s, working and living a full life, despite his illness. Thanks to the marvelous sports tournament in his honour, thousands of other victims of those cruel diseases will also lead longer and more productive lives, possibly someday even beating the illnesses completely.

And the Robbie International Soccer Tournament? In the early summer of 1988 it hosted some 250 teams, including entries from across Canada, the United States, Taiwan, and the Philippines. As the *Scar-*

These boats paint a tranquil setting at the marina. Photo by Glen Jones

borough Mirror, one of its proud sponsors, once editorialized, "The Robbie is something we should all feel good about. It brings out the best in young people, in athletes, in their parents. It's a major contribution."

Scarborough is also home to one of the most modern and attractive multi-sport complexes in the world serving disabled and deserving youth. Visiting the handsome gymnasium at Variety Village Sport Training and Fitness Centre, out on the east Danforth, one might honestly wonder if any of those ecstatic children are disabled in any way. They play tennis and volleyball, and toss shotputs and discuses as well as any "able-bodied" children. "It's not until you ask them to do some kind of physical activity that they can't do, that you realize they have a disability," programme supervisor Cyril Gibbs commented recently. "You zero-in on the disability and then you work around it. Despite their so-called disabilities, they're not too limited. There are a number of things they can do."

Tens of thousands watch and contribute to the annual Variety Club Telethon, which in its 1988 edition—starring such major Canadian-cum-international stars as Monty Hall, Lloyd Bochner, Ronnie Hawkins, Maureen Forrester, Burton Cummings, and Peter Appleyard, and such prominent visitors as Tony Bennett—raised over $3.7 million for Variety Village. Tent 28 of the Variety Club of Ontario also raises money for the sports centre.

Its new Aquatics wing, a $5.7-million project, opened in late 1988, and features a unique 40-metre, six-lane teaching/training pool. Over 1,000 special-education children from school boards across Metro Toronto use its 70,000-square-foot fieldhouse for physical education classes every week, and there are summer camps as well. There are daily aerobic classes, fencing, and a unique "self-help" workroom, equipped with dual-height working surfaces for special repairs, modifications, and service to standard and racing wheelchairs. There are summer sports camps, the annual Lieutenant-Governor's Invitational Games, Variety Village Jr. Championships, and more.

Keith Brettell, 16, is in Grade 10 and has spina bifida, so he moves

A wide range of activities for young and old can be found in Scarborough. Courtesy, City of Scarborough

about in a wheelchair. His sports include 10-km road racing, track, basketball, weightlifting, and swimming. When his mother Pat is asked what he was like before his sports activities, Keith interrupts. "I used to be a real loner, right, Mum?" His mother nods in agreement. "I was continually on the outside of the crowd," the teen continues. "I never felt I belonged." Today he does, as do thousands of other youngsters across Metro Toronto, thanks to Scarborough's Variety Village.

In late 1987, it was announced that the fourth YMCA to be built in Metropolitan Toronto would be in downtown Scarborough. Officials claimed it would be the best one yet.

The YMCA expects the new $15-million complex will have close to 7,000 members the first year it opens. George Rodger, the vice president of financial development for the YMCA, has been quoted as saying that "this one will have the nicest family programme [of the Ys] in North America." Added YMCA governor Steve Gilchrist, "This will be a facility like no other in the community of Metropolitan Toronto. Its design features will be award-winners."

Which would be fitting, since the full-service building, with its day-care, restaurant, squash courts, dance studio, indoor track, meeting rooms, swimming pools, and other related social and health services will be right next to the Scarborough City Hall—another award-winner.

Scarborough is bursting with activities for literally everyone in the community, as well as across Metro Toronto, and—thanks to its various international tournaments—North America and the entire world.

But there's much more, too. The Scarborough Lacrosse Association is growing by literal leaps and bounds. The Scarborough United Women's Soccer Club's under-18 team, the Dynamos, won a Canadian record-setting fourth consecutive national championship in the fall of 1987, with a win over the Calgary Chinooks.

The Scarborough Olympic Wrestling Club came back from Prince Albert, Saskatchewan, in the spring of 1987, with the Canadian schoolboy (bantam) wrestling title.

And Scarborough has become, as well, "a hotbed of snooker activity," according to recent reports in the press.

By 1990, a new all-season recreation facility will open on an old landfill site at Meadowvale Road, north of Sheppard Avenue. The new park will include beginner, intermediate, and advanced downhill ski slopes, cross-country skiing, horseback-riding trails, and a hang-gliding launch pad. A scenic lookout will also be built. Furthermore, if insurance coverage can be obtained, the hang-gliding facility there should be the best in all of southern Ontario, according to experts. Colorado and the Alps had better watch out. Scarborough is moving up.

As recently as 1987, a wide-ranging telephone survey was completed by the Planning Team of the Recreation and Parks Department, interviewing men and women in some 1,400 households. The results were most informative, indicating "a dramatic increase in demand for . . . more adult-oriented sports facilities," and "increasing interest in the out-of-doors, the natural environment, and physical and emotional well-being . . ."

The report also noted that "Scarborough is fortunate in its range of amenities. The city boasts a full spectrum of open space and parks, an excellent variety of parks facilities and an enviable complement of sports and leisure buildings."

But Scarborough has no plans to slow down. As part of its recommendations for its master plan, the report declared, "Scarborough is a well-served community, is financially secure, has an optimistic future and is growing. Its recreation and leisure resources are adequate in terms of traditional recreation but change and growth are clearly indicated to meet changing demands . . ."

This was then followed by a number of pages of suggestions, ranging from more trails and pathways for bicycling and cross-country skiing, to more parks, programming for teens and seniors, etc.

For the able-bodied, the disabled, the participant, and the observer, Scarborough's recreational opportunities are always increasing. Scarborough has given new meaning to the phrase "being a good sport."

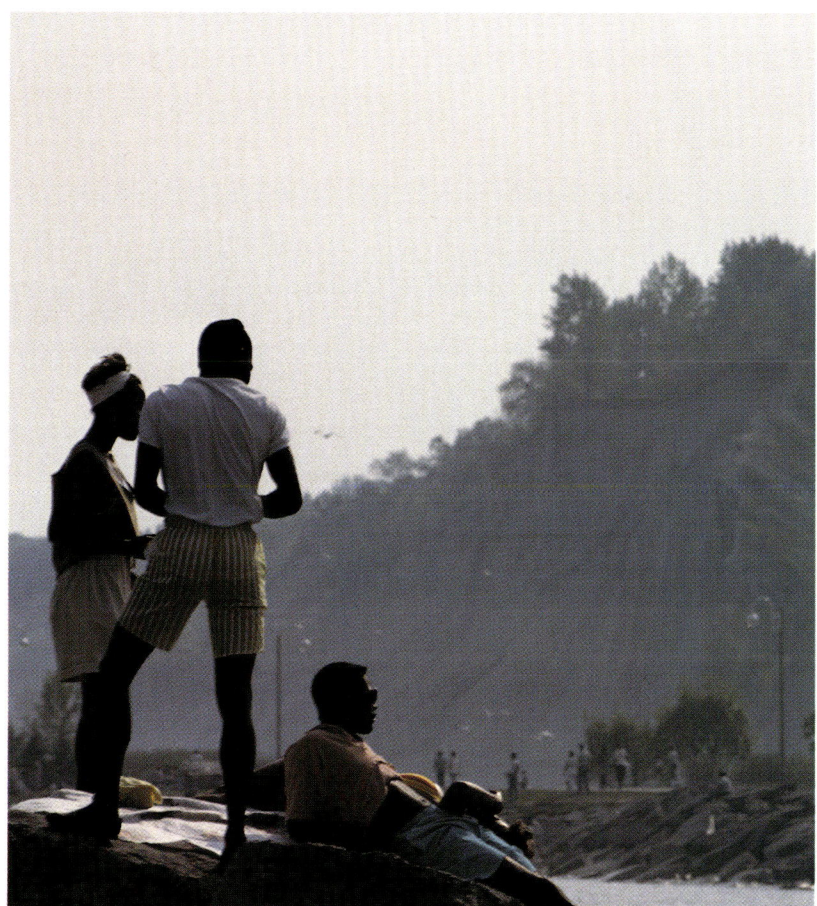

Strollers enjoy the view from Scarborough Bluffs. Photo by Dawn Goss/ First Light

CHAPTER FOUR

The World-Class Metro Toronto Zoo

Very few cities in the world could honestly dedicate a full chapter to their zoo, but Scarborough is most assuredly one of them. Open to the public since the summer of 1974, the Metro Toronto Zoo was sited in Scarborough for the same reason the city continues to thrive and grow: It has more land available than any other city or borough in the Metropolitan Toronto area.

So when a group of 150 zoologists from across North America visited our zoo in the early 1980s, the response was not at all surprising.

"It's fantastic!" declared the supervisor for the Busch Gardens Zoo in Williamsburg, Virginia. "It's something for everybody else to shoot for in the years to come. Your zoo is leading the way—years ahead of everybody, from what I've seen."

"Yeah, I guess we want to copy it. We're not proud," admitted the zoologist and curator for the up-and-coming Syracuse zoo. "We've been looking at different zoos but sent our staff up here because this is one of the premier zoos in the world."

An educational consultant for zoos exclaimed, "I'm in love! The whole physical setting of this place is breathtaking."

At the end of that four-hour tour—although most visitors find that it takes several days to really get a sense of the zoo—the experts agreed there were three factors making the Scarborough gem a King of the Jungle:

*Unlike every other zoo in major cities around the world, the one in Scarborough still has hundreds of acres for expansion.

*The zoo has an open concept, using moats or acrylic to confine animals, rather than cages.

*The animals are grouped according to geography rather than species.

Indeed, less than 10 years after the zoo opened its doors in Scarborough, the *New York Times* ranked this zoo one of the top 10 on the planet.

It wasn't always this way, of course. From the late 1880s until 1973, the main zoo in the Toronto area was squashed into five hectares in Riverdale, near the Don Valley, on the edge of downtown. It was a traditional nineteenth-century zoo, small and cramped, although not without its charm. But the animals were stuck behind barred cages, which may still be the norm in the vast majority of the world's zoos, but it seems almost barbaric after experiencing Scarborough.

In 1966, the Metropolitan Toronto Zoological Society formed to develop a new zoo. It was immediately clear what the ideal site would be, and it is worth quoting from the zoo's official history:

From this study of three sites, the Citizens' Advisory Committee chose the beautiful Glen Rouge area of Scarborough . . . The site, on land owned by the Metro Toronto and Region Conservation Authority, is one of the most beautiful in the Metro Toronto region. It consists of 300 acres of tableland

Flamingos add a flamboyant touch of colour to the zoo. Photo by Glen Jones

Above: This exotic crane is one of the many attractions at the Metro Toronto Zoo. Photo by Glen Jones

Above right: Giraffes are a favorite at any zoo, and Scarborough's is no exception. Photo by Barry Dursley/First Light

Right: This polar bear makes a demand at the Toronto Zoo. Photo by Glen Jones

formed by the Rouge River on the west and the Little Rouge River on the east, and 410 acres of land in the river valleys. A heavily wooded hill in the centre of the tableland forms a divide between two distinctly different terrains. The west side tends to be rolling and hilly, while the east side is flat. The central woods consist of a magnificent virgin stand of sugar maples, beech, oak, birch and aspen.

The master plan was approved in 1969 by Metropolitan Council, of which the then borough of Scarborough was a proud and active member, with a $22 million allocation, and the zoo opened less than five years later. With the multi-million-dollar expansion plan now in force, few doubt that the Metro Toronto Zoo will be in the top three when the next international survey of zoos is taken by the *New York Times*.

Since August 15, 1974, Scarborough has been home to this magnificent zoo. As we have noted, no other metropolitan area in the world would have had 287 hectares to spare.

But size in itself would mean little without inspired planning. For instance, there is an important science called zoogeography, the study of animal distribution, and it is done to perfection at the Metro Zoo.

All the animals and plants at the zoo have been grouped according to where they are found in the wild. This seems obvious, but it is rarely attempted in the world's zoos, whether because of lack of foresight or lack of space.

The Metro Zoo is divided into five zoogeographic regions: Africa, the Americas, Australasia, Eurasia, and Indo-Malaya, which represent the broad ecological divisions of the earth's animal population. These zoogeographic regions can be distinguished, because while animals tend to disperse widely across the earth's surface, they always come up against natural barriers such as rivers, oceans, and mountain ranges, which stop them in their tracks.

The African Pavilion promises wonders from the veldt. Photo by Glen Jones

An orangutan and his mother enjoy prestigious and comfortable accommodations at the Metro Toronto Zoo. Courtesy, City of Scarborough

Visitors stroll toward the Indo-Malayan Pavilion. Photo by Glen Jones

The Metro Zoo does not only show off its animals, but displays them in their native environments. This means re-creating, as much as possible, the natural environments of the animals. These range from equatorial rainforest to woodland, from swamp to desert.

The creation of such naturalistic settings demanded a world-class botanical collection, now including over 400 trees, 4,000 shrubs, and an almost-endless groundcovering of plants, today valued at over $5 million. The stunning indoor pavilions include such unusual plants as a banyan tree, weighing in at more than three tonnes; a sausage tree, whose kielbasa-shaped fruit hangs from two-metre-long cords; the edible fig tree; and the only living baobab tree in Canada. The Metro Zoo also has the most varied palm collection in the country and a large collection of exotic orchids, as well.

So much for the quite extraordinary plants; what of the zoo's animal collection? Nearly 4,000 animals live on the premises, representing more than 440 different species of life.

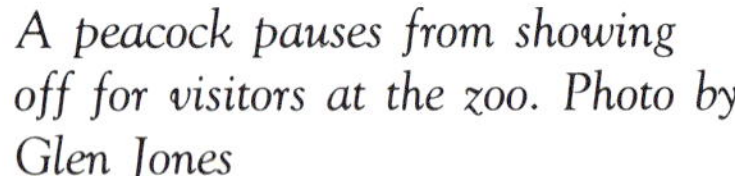

A peacock pauses from showing off for visitors at the zoo. Photo by Glen Jones

These Bactrian camels are in quarantine. Photo by Stephen Homer/First Light

This deer is tagged for identification purposes at the Metro Toronto Zoo. Photo by Stephen Homer/First Light

The zoo's population changes every single day, of course. This is a list of just some of the babies born at the Metro Zoo during six weeks in May and June 1982:

Six wood bison. Five reindeer. Six mouflon wild sheep. One Indian fruit bat. Five Bactrian camels. Five Arctic wolves. Four aoudads, which are Barbary sheep. Two gemsbok, which are African antelopes. One European bison. Two mara, which are South American rodents. One patas monkey. Eleven white-tailed deer. Nine Mandarin ducks. Three Barbary apes. Two African fur seals. Six mute swans. Two Himalayan tahr. One sacred ibis. Three beavers.

During 1984, to take a typical year in this very fruitful-and-multiplying zoo, there were over 1,000 animal births, nearly 40 percent of which were mammals. Metro Zoo has had outstanding success in breeding a number of endangered species, including the Lowland gorilla, Sumatran orangutan, and the African elephant, which is a source of pride to zoologists everywhere, as well as everyone who loves animals and cares for the future of this planet.

This astounding fertility has never slowed over the years, and has even increased. The July/August 1987 newsletter of the Metropolitan Toronto Zoological Society reported that in the spring of that year, "hundreds of mammals entered the world" at the zoo, including "25 kowari, six Bennett's wallabies, three Egyptian fruit bats, a mara, four dwarf rabbits, two red-bellied marmosets, a Japanese macaque, a Hamadryas baboon, three Chinese leopards, three Reeve's muntjacs, a sitatunga, five reindeer, one Damara and one Grevy's zebra, seven

This zoo employee prepares some of the food the animals consume at the Metro Toronto Zoo. The animals eat more than a million kilograms of food a year. Photo by Stephen Homer/First Light

Facing page, top: A Bengal tiger rests outside the Australasian Pavilion, one of the zoo's authentic habitats. Photo by Glen Jones

Facing page, bottom left: These Japanese macaques form a touching family portrait at the Metro Toronto Zoo. Photo by Stephen Homer/First Light

Nubian ibex, 12 West Caucasian tur," and so on.

Furthermore, the zoo turned Scarborough into a world centre of zoological study. Endangered and difficult-to-breed animal species may be saved from extinction by the test tube technology currently being developed at Metro. Thanks to the Blackstock Fellowship, the Metro Zoo brought in Dr. Karen Goodrowe from Washington, D.C., where she had been responsible for the first test-tube kitten ever born. Dr. Goodrowe is currently delving into the breeding habits of such endangered species as the Lowland gorilla, kowari, Tasmanian devils, and marmosets, and hopes to add thousands more to the already long list of animals born and bred in the Metro Zoo.

All decent zoos have the old standards: the lions, tigers, giraffes, elephants, bears, and monkeys. But within a few short years, the zoo in Scarborough has obtained the Tasmanian devil; the rat kangaroo, or bettong; the Echidna, or spiny anteater, which looks like a porcupine and is one of the only two mammals on earth that lay eggs; the extremely rare snow leopard; the endangered Indian rhino; over 30 species of parrots; the alligator snapping turtle, which is the largest freshwater turtle in captivity; the endangered Malayan bonytongue fish; and, as noted above, some 4,000 more animals.

Because the aim of the zoo has been to show the animals in their native environments, considerable imagination went into the design. Public walkways, for example, are at varying levels, allowing the animals to be seen from many different viewpoints. Even the organic form of the pavilions has an exterior profile which flows naturally into the surrounding landscape. The restaurants and service buildings, impressively, were designed with a similar sensitivity, and the entire zoo's access for the disabled is among the best in the world.

The Metro Toronto Zoo is a stunning creation, and truly the crown of Scarborough's many attractions. And it provides funny and fascinating trivia:

*The animals require over one million kilograms of food per year. Twice a week, the commissary staff prepares more than 600 kilograms of meat.

*In a single year, one adult gorilla—and the zoo has many—will devour 512 kilograms of monkey chow; 365 hard-boiled eggs; 365 kilograms of celery; 158 kilograms of lettuce; 146 kilograms of carrots; 120 kilograms of hydroponic sprouts; 82 kilograms of bananas; 73 kilograms of oranges; 73 kilograms of tomatoes; 68 yams; 63 kilograms of cabbage; 52 sugar cane stalks; 30 kilograms of cottage cheese; 30 coconuts; 28 kilograms of green beans; 10 kilograms of yogurt; 5 kilograms of peanuts; 4 kilograms of figs; 3 kilograms of raisins; and 2 kilograms of dates.

*Every year, the Metro Zoo feeds its animal collection 900,000 mealworms; 550,000 kilograms of commercial feed; 300,000 crickets; 25,000 mice; 22,000 bales of hay; and 20,000 kilograms of frozen fish. In a single year, these animals pay the zoo back with over 1,000 tonnes of manure, which the zoo uses in production of its own fertilizer, which it markets under the name of "Zoo Poo."

*In recent years, the zoo has witnessed brain surgery on a baby gorilla, root canal work on a snow leopard, orthopedic surgery on the legs of a mandrill, and the repairing of a giraffe's broken jaw. And when a macho West Caucasian tur broke a horn in a battle for herd dominance, the zoo's maintenance staff helped out the veterinarians by making a splint out of two-by-fours and muffler clamps.

*Maintenance came through on another interesting occasion, when an agave plant decided to move into rare bloom, shooting up a 10-metre flower stalk. The staff made a hole in the roof of the Americas Pavilion in the dead of winter, and built an acrylic tent, which allowed the bud to open safely.

Above: This baby rhino began life at the Metro Toronto Zoo. More than 1,000 animal babies are born each year at the zoo. Photo by Glen Jones

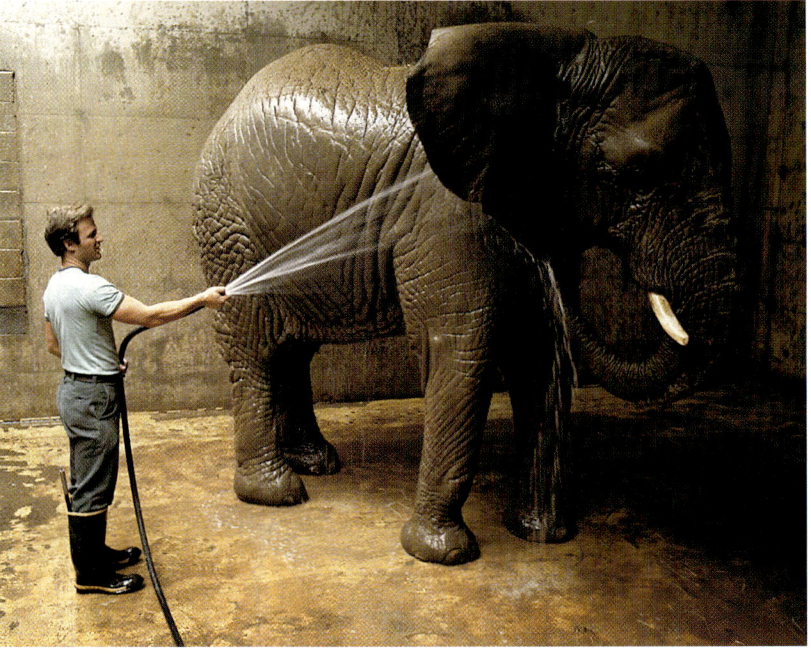

This elephant enjoys a shower at the Metro Toronto Zoo. Photo by Stephen Homer/First Light

This falcon is among the incredible wildlife featured at the Zoo. Photo by Glen Jones

*Five million litres of water per week are used for everyday needs such as watering the animals. These, in turn, eagerly water back, since the elephants use over 3,000 litres of water every day of the year.

*Always innovative, the Metro Zoo created a special light cycle in an extension of the Australasian Pavilion, in December 1983. By reversing day and night, zoo designers allowed visitors to experience the sights and sounds of the Tasmanian devil, the hairy-nosed wombat, and the spiny anteater.

*The 162 hectares of the Rouge River Valley allow the zoo to maintain large groups of individual species much as they occur in the wild. White-tailed deer, woodland caribou, Arctic wolves, Dall's sheep, wood bison, wapiti and musk oxen roam free year-round in the Canadian Animal Domain, watched eagerly by the hundreds of thousands riding the monorail quietly and unobtrusively through the massive area.

In addition to the wonderful areas where animals run free, or near-free, there are the exquisitely beautiful pavilions sprinkled throughout the Metro Toronto Zoo. Each is climate-controlled and enclosed, filled with remarkable botanical gardens and the occasional bird flapping around one's head. That huge banyan tree is in the Indo-Malayan Pavilion, along with giant rubber, mango, and umbrella trees. The African Pavilion features a gorgeous fan-shaped traveller's palm from Madagascar. And the jasmine with their perfumed flowers in the Eurasian Pavilion defy description.

The zoo features several walking tours, each trail clearly marked with fun-to-follow, brightly coloured, sasquatch-sized footprints. And such delightful attractions as Littlefoot Land, just north of the main gate, allow children to touch and feed rabbits, sheep, goats, donkeys, and even camels. Polar bear and cape fur seal feedings are often hilarious, and bird demonstrations fascinate visitors with the flying and hunting skills of such species as the red-tailed hawk, kestrel, and great horned owl.

Scarborough has so many attractions to be proud of, and one of the world's most exciting and dynamic zoos is merely one of them. Another is Zooski, cross-country skiing offered at the zoo during the winter months. Three groomed, colour-coded trails, each geared to a different skill level, allow skiers to travel through Africa, Eurasia, and the Canadian Animal Domain.

Attractions like these have brought more than 20,000 members into the Metropolitan Toronto Zoological Society, many of them Scarborough residents. Regular courses on such subjects as "The Wolf: Fact or Fiction," "Venomous Reptiles," and "Those Amazing Plants," as well as Zoo Camp ("Send your child on safari in deepest darkest Scarborough this summer"), and pandas from China and koalas from the San Diego Zoo, have brought more than 1.5 million visitors to the zoo. With approximately 250 staff year-round and an extra 100 during the summers, the Metro Toronto Zoo is a major Scarborough business, as well, adding over $10 million a year to the city's burgeoning economy.

Most extraordinary of all, the zoo is situated just a few kilometres east of the Scarborough City Centre. It's no accident; the zoo lies within Scarborough's boundaries. Like the Metro Toronto Zoo, Scarborough is educational, beautiful, ever promising, and ever expanding. Thanks to its zoo, South America, Europe, Asia, and Africa are only a few minutes away.

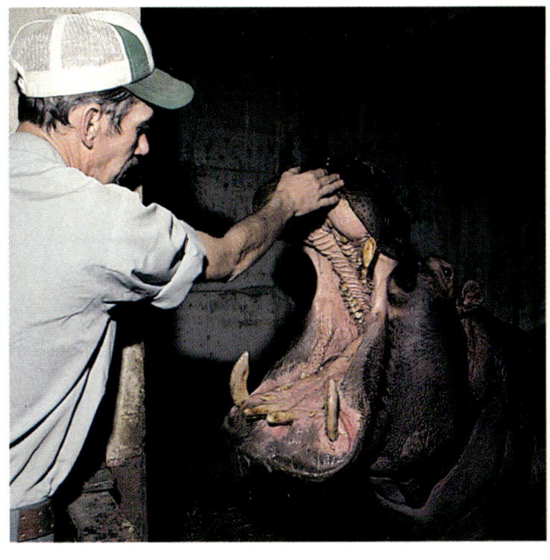

Above: This hippo smiles broadly for the camera at the Metro Toronto Zoo. Photo by Stephen Homer/First Light

Left: A keeper feeds a baby gorilla. This little guy's appetite will grow as he does. Photo by Stephen Homer/First Light

CHAPTER FIVE

The Arts in These Parts

*don't know art, but I know what I like* is an old cliché with little meaning in Scarborough, where a large and growing number of men and women who do know art—and even create it—have come to live, work, and enjoy culture.

Arts have always been available in Scarborough, of course, despite those who mock the city as a cultural wasteland. The mockery is understandable, if not acceptable or fair, since Scarborough is, after all, a younger and more recently developed part of a very exciting metropolitan area. So, not unlike the boroughs of Brooklyn and Queens, both bursting with arts but ever in the shadow of a cultural mecca like Manhattan, Scarborough has similarly suffered snide condescension.

In recent years, however, Scarborough's arts community has matured—partly, thanks to Arts Scarborough, a strong and forceful voice for artists. Arts Scarborough is an umbrella group whose activities encompass every art form in the city. Formed over a decade ago, in 1978, it is funded by such municipal, provincial, and federal patrons as Metro Toronto, the Ontario Arts Council, the City of Scarborough itself, the Ontario Ministry of Citizenship and Culture, Canada Employment Programs, and corporate and private donors. It also both supports and publicizes the Scarborough Board of Education's efforts to develop the arts.

The City of Scarborough deserves its reputation for welcoming artists. In the Great Depression, Rosa and Spencer Clark opened the Guild of All Arts, which quickly became a haven—even a lifesaver—for craftspeople during those difficult years. The Guild Inn, now run commercially, still provides studio space for several artists, and supports a full-time sculptor-in-residence.

Not that the Guild Inn is the only game in town. Tucked away in a quiet corner of the city is one of Scarborough's most precious cultural resources, Cedar Ridge Creative Centre. It grew out of a studio school originated by the same supportive Clarks. Potters, painters, weavers, and woodcarvers come to Cedar Ridge to hone their skills. More than a school, Cedar Ridge's large rooms and park-like setting make it fine for creating as well as displaying both arts and crafts. Classes are small—usually a dozen or less—and the teachers (and occasional top-notch lecturers, such as world-renowned wildlife artist Glen Loates) are widely admired. Since 1985, the city of Scarborough took over administration and gallery programming, one more example of how this municipality supports cultural activities.

Yet even if Scarborough did not put out such a welcome mat for those in the arts, the city still would be a very attractive place to create. The former executive director of Arts Scarborough, Lynne B. Atkinson, who coordinated the entertainment programme for the British Columbia Pavilion at Expo '86, addressed this question in Arts Scarborough's magazine:

Could Scarborough become a home base for Metro's arts community? Arts Scarborough thinks so. [Look at] the problems faced by artists downtown in the

Ornate architecture characterizes the buildings at the Guild Inn. Courtesy, City of Scarborough

Above: The Guild Inn provides studio space for artists and supports a full-time sculptor-in-residence. Courtesy, City of Scarborough

Right: Gardens stretch impressively toward the lovely Guild Inn. Photo by Dawn Goss/First Light

Above: Students learn traditional folk art techniques at Cedar Ridge. Courtesy, City of Scarborough

Left: Built in 1932, the Guild Inn houses the beautiful Sculpture Garden, offers art exhibits, and has a collection of historical architecture, saved from some of Toronto's finest buildings. Photo by Glen Jones

face of rising rents and plunging vacancy rates. In short, artists, like many other lower-income workers, are being pushed out of the heart of major metropolitan areas.

This is bad news for Toronto, much of whose reputation as a tourist centre rests on the liveliness of its arts scene. It can be good news for Scarborough, however, if this city is willing to make a commitment to encouraging artists to live and work here.

There is no hard and fast rule that limits arts districts to downtown areas. All that artists need, besides a flourishing arts community to provide creative support and inspiration, is affordable work and living space. Scarborough, by providing the latter, can contribute to the development of the former.

And, the city notes with some pride, Arts Scarborough has been busy for a full decade now, making the city a better place to enjoy and create art. It offers guest speakers on culture, art shows, counselling on grants and other artistic opportunities, publicity of events in a monthly newsletter, and even an arts directory.

In this way, both the artist and the public have gained. Arts Scarborough's more than 800 members help enrich the entire community through art events, volunteer programmes, a computerized resource centre, art rental and sales, and much more. And it is growing by leaps and bounds.

Recent headlines in the *Toronto Star* suggest the importance of the organization. "Arts Scarborough Will Sponsor Workshop for Novice Writers," reads one. "Arts Scarborough Holds Arts Show at the Consilium" is another. "Scarborough's Writing Community Alive & Well," proclaims a third.

What are some examples of the artistic organizations and artists that have made Scarborough an even more pleasant place to live? Here are just a few examples:

The Scarborough Philharmonic

The Scarborough Philharmonic Orchestra was founded in 1980, and consists of some 55 musicians, most of them residents of the city. Although the majority of the musicians are non-professional, they manage to sell out many of the half-dozen or so concerts they give each year in a high school auditorium.

Although the orchestra has had some hard economic times, things have been looking up since experienced conductor and Scarborough resident Christopher Kitts was hired in 1985.

The SPO performs a free Christmas concert each year at the Scarborough Civic Centre and is rapidly becoming a precious part of the community. Scholarships are available to help musicians improve their abilities, and with each year, more and more city residents are taking advantage of the opportunity to hear their own symphony, consisting of their neighbours.

Cathedral Bluffs Symphony Orchestra

Scarborough even has another orchestra. Cathedral Bluffs Symphony Orchestra was formed in 1985, and has performed to acclaim since then. It features about five dozen musicians, most of them residents of the city, and maestro Clifford Poole, a professor at the Royal Conservatory of Music. Cathedral Bluffs musicians range from retirees to young music students, and they have treated their fellow Scarboroughites to fine classical music for several years. The symphony presents five subscription concerts each season at a city high school, and each concert features a talented guest performer.

There is also a Cathedral Bluffs String Quartet, composed of orchestra members, and, like the city's older symphony, it financially supports aspiring young students with a bursary. The CBSO plays a free Accent on Youth Concert each September.

Scarborough Theatre Guild

For three decades, the Scarborough Theatre Guild has been "promoting entertainment," in the words of its business manager and past president Norma Francis. And four times a year, in early fall, before Christmas, in March, and in May, the Guild presents its excellent fare. There are 60 members in the group, doing everything from performing to designing and painting sets.

With theatre tickets in downtown Toronto ranging up to $50 a seat, it is a pleasure to find such competent performances in one's own neighbourhood. And, unlike the harsher world of professional theatre, the Scarborough Theatre Guild extends its hand to local high school students interested in careers in the field. Guild members teach them backstage jobs and allow them to observe rehearsals and see productions take shape. It's not Broadway, but it is thrilling to the teenaged apprentices, the performers, and the audiences as well. As Ms. Francis proclaims, "We give our patrons a reasonable night's entertainment for much less money."

Irish Choral Society

In keeping with Scarborough's ethnic mix, the Irish Choral Society is fully 40 percent non-Irish—including its president, Arthur Hall.

The society was founded in 1961 so people of Irish origin could get together and sing songs of their homeland. They have since expanded their repertoire to include Scottish, English, Canadian, and American traditional songs, as well.

Three dozen singers now perform regularly at senior citizens' homes, legion halls, hospitals, and, naturally, at the Scarborough Civic Centre and Town Centre. Declares its president, "I don't think there are too many similar choral groups. What we offer the public is excellence in four-part harmony singing of traditional songs."

Scarborough Bluffs Orchestra is seen here in performance. Courtesy, Scarborough Chamber of Commerce

Hollywood's latest is on view at the Scarborough Village Theatre. Photo by Glen Jones

The Scarborough Choral Society

The oldest performing arts group in the city recently performed on its 35th anniversary. The Scarborough Choral Society's first incarnation was as the Knox Presbyterian Church Choir in 1952, presenting Gilbert and Sullivan's *Trial by Jury.* In 1961, it took on its more secular name, and moved to the 1,100-seat Cedarbrae Collegiate, to accommodate a larger cast, a 35-piece orchestra, and ever-increasing audiences. Over the years, the Scarborough Choral Society has presented major musicals each March, Christmas concerts each December, and has supported numerous charities. Whether with *Die Fledermaus* or Gilbert and Sullivan, the SCS entertains thousands of the city's residents every year.

One could spend another hundred pages talking about Scarborough's other artistic and cultural groups, such as the Scarborough Music Theatre, presenting fine productions of Broadway musicals and Gilbert and Sullivan operas for over a quarter-century.

Or the 22 horn players, 18 percussionists, and 12 flag and rifle twirlers of the two-decades-old Cardinals Drum and Bugle Corps of Scarborough.

Not to mention the excellent Amadeus Choir of Scarborough, The Art Guild of Scarborough, The Scarborough Quilters Guild, The Scarborough Players, and the annual Children's Festival at Woodside Square.

The Scarborough chapter of Sweet Adelines has been singing sweetly since 1956. Today, there are nearly 80 women members, ranging in age from their early 20s to late 60s. They twice won international honours for best Sweet Adelines chorus, and entertain their fellow residents by the thousands.

The Scarborough Dukes of Harmony are also winners. The mustachioed gentlemen are past International Chorus champions and in 1986 won the Ontario District Barbershop Chorus Competition. Today, they have over 130 active members, who have no cause to hide in the shower when they sing their delightful songs. Indeed, they recently performed at a major concert in Roy Thomson Hall, *The Best of Barbershop.*

For a city which was but a tiny township just a few decades ago, Scarborough has come a very long way. It even reveres its share of cultural heroes and institutions. For example, the very gifted painter Doris McCarthy recently won the Order of Canada for her excellent art. Ed Bickert and Peter Appleyard are both internationally known musicians. Simon Ng recently won the Canadian Gold and Silver Medal for magazine illustration. The city is also justifiably proud of its symphonies, theatre guilds, writing clubs, dancers, and weavers.

It's all part of Scarborough's charm. The city bursts with amateur, semi-professional, and professional arts, entertainment, and culture; activities which are too often neglected in a much larger municipal area. Neglected, and even ignored.

Other forms of popular culture have blossomed within the expansive city limits of Scarborough, as well. Today there are fully three dozen movie theatres in the city, meaning that its residents no longer have to go elsewhere to the movies. And with such popular nightclubs as Bennigan's, Victoria's, Solitaire's, B.B. McGee's, and The Falcon's Nest sprinkled across the city, there are even fewer reasons for Scarboroughites to leave town.

Scarborough is a great place to work and live, and thanks to a strong and vital artistic, cultural, and social life, supported by business, government, and the public at large, it is a good place to play, as well.

CHAPTER SIX

The Education Boom

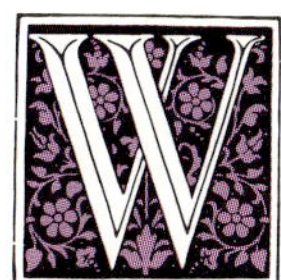

ith Scarborough's massive growth in population and housing since the end of the Second World War, the city's public school system became one of the biggest north of the 49th parallel. In fact, it is now the largest public school board in all of Metropolitan Toronto, and the fifth largest in all of Canada.

As of the fall of 1988 there were over 130 elementary schools in the city and another two dozen secondary schools, serving over 76,000 students in total. The Scarborough Board of Education employs around 4,400 teaching staff and another 2,400 non-teaching support staff, ranging from psychologists, social workers, and counsellors to clerical workers and caretakers. This huge number has made the board into one of the 20 largest employers in all of Metro.

And, in keeping with the unique dual-support system of the province of Ontario, a Metropolitan Separate School Board provides a Catholic education for over 22,000 students in over four dozen elementary and secondary schools in the city.

As with so many other aspects of its community, from transportation to health to parks, Scarborough's Board of Education has been a leader among school boards in the entire country in curriculum development. This is no small matter; for while the Ministry of Education of the province of Ontario issues general guidelines to every one of its many school boards, the Scarborough Board of Education has long insisted on developing its own curriculum guides. Furthermore, while many school boards employ only one or two coordinators responsible for various subject areas, Scarborough has a coordinator for every single one. Indeed, this insistence on originality and excellence has led many boards across the province to purchase and use the superb curricula developed by the Scarborough board. Imitation is the sincerest form of flattery, and to have thousands of students across the province of Ontario getting a better education because of the creativity of Scarborough educators is the most satisfying flattery of all.

These quality guides are not merely handed out to Scarborough principals and teachers with the hope that they will be put to good use. In the mid-1980s, the Scarborough Board of Education embarked on its important Curriculum Development and Implementation Programme, in which hundreds of teachers and principals work together with the board to ensure that these superior curricula are being used correctly in the classrooms. In this way, the board maintains consistent standards throughout the system, and Joanna in School X in northeast Scarborough takes the same excellent courses as Johnny in School Y, down in the southwest part of the city.

For many years now, the Scarborough Board of Education has also had a good "laid-on" excursion programme, which means that every child, from the first grade on up, will go on some kind of enrichment journey each year, whether visiting a farm, Black Creek Pioneer Village, the Ontario Science Centre, or the city's superb zoo. They can also enjoy such excellent programmes as the Hillside Outdoor Education School in Scarborough, for elementary students, and the

It's easy to see why the Scarborough campus of the University of Toronto is the first choice for many students. Photo by Dawn Goss/ First Light

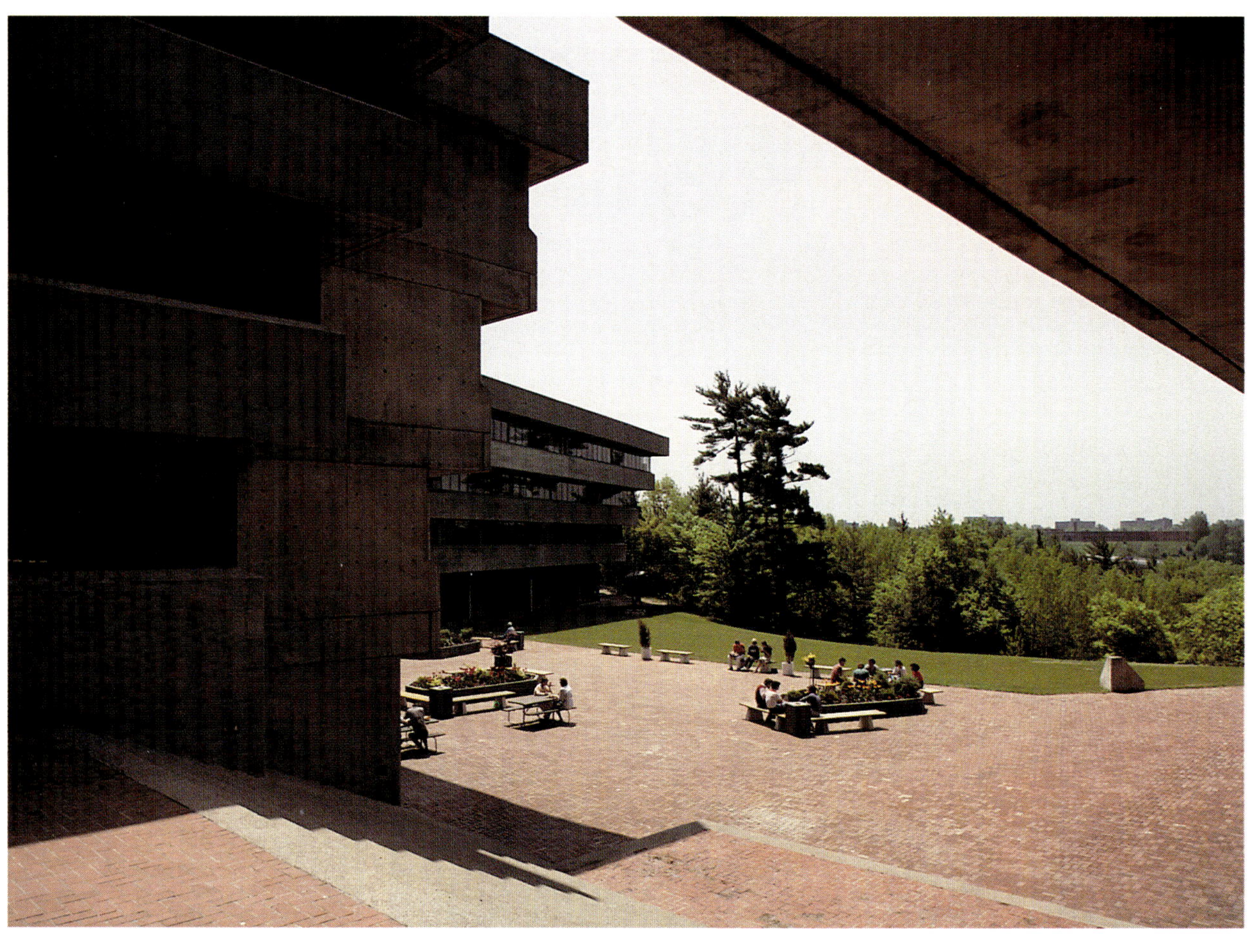

Above: The Scarborough campus of the University of Toronto serves over 5,000 students from around the world, and has a faculty of more than 200. Photo by Peter Tang/ First Light

Right: St. Augustine Seminary holds its own when it comes to architectural elegance. Photo by Jack Holman

Scarborough Outdoor Education School in Kearney, Ontario, for students in grade six and beyond. Schools apply to have their youngsters attend, and there are classes every day of the week, year-round. "These are model facilities," they point out at the Scarborough board, "where students get a flavour of what it's like to both live in the wilderness and study it."

In a country that has two official languages, it is crucial that students get a solid knowledge of both, which is why the French Immersion Programme in the Scarborough schools is one of the most admired and copied in all of Canada. Robert McConnell is the coordinator of modern languages for the board, and has been responsible for developing this vital concept across the country. Indeed, McConnell is considered one of the leaders of French immersion anywhere, and has co-written the majority of the textbooks used from the elementary through the secondary school levels in Canada and even internationally.

Scarborough has a wonderfully diverse population, which is why its board of education recently published a Race Relations, Ethnic Relations, and Multicultural Policy—one of the first in Canada to do this. Although Scarborough's schools have long had innovative programmes for English as a Second Language (ESL) to help recent immigrants to the country, they also feature such interesting programmes as SMILE (Scarborough Multicultural Interschool Leadership Experience) and GRACE (Graduate Race-Relations Awareness and Community Experience), which assist students in increasing their self-esteem and in developing leadership.

Scarborough Board of Education is also one of the first boards in the country to publish and publicize a values statement establishing the

Above: It's time to go home at Lord Roberts Public School. Photo by Dawn Goss/First Light

Above left: This bus pulls up to Lord Roberts Public School. Photo by Peter Tang/First Light

Below: These kids relax on the grounds of Heather Heights Junior High School. Photo by Glen Jones

goals and priorities of education. The statement confirms the importance of personal and social development of every student, and stresses the development of respect and caring for oneself and others. This values statement has gone out to all teachers, staff, and students in Scarborough, and brochures and posters have been posted throughout the city, demonstrating that the school system offers its students more than just a dozen years of academic schooling.

Scarborough schools also have the largest "co-operative programme" in the entire country, in which several thousand students are assigned each year to work-stations in businesses and industries across Metro Toronto, gaining credits while spending months learning about work in the "real world."

Scarborough's Education in the Workplace (EWP) is also laudable. It is a service operated for the community by language instruction specialists at the Scarborough Board of Education, offering assistance to business, industry, government, and labour organizations that employ immigrant workers who are not fluent in English. In co-operation with employers and employee groups, EWP staff both design and deliver language classes at the workplace for workers and supervisory

The Scarborough Centre for Alternative Studies is an adult re-entry programme enabling any adult to attend any secondary school in the city. Photo by Glen Jones

staff. In the words of Donald Ablett, the director of corporate planning at Brown Manufacturing, Ltd., in Scarborough, "The EWP programme has been tremendous for us. The employees developed greater confidence in their English skills, enabling them to participate more fully in an English-language society. The company wins through better communication and productivity."

The Scarborough Centre for Alternative Studies is another way Scarborough reaches out to the "real world." It is an adult re-entry programme for mature students, in which any adult from the age of 19 up can attend any secondary school in Scarborough, whether in segregated classes, or integrated with high school teenagers.

The Scarborough Board of Education has also provided outstanding enrichment and gifted programmes for many years. Saturday morning Math Enrichment classes, and others for the gifted in Visual Arts, have been available since the 1970s. And the large number of students who have won such major, Canada-wide math competitions as the Euclid, Descartes, Caley, and Fermat contests suggests just how successful these programmes have been. In fact, Scarborough students are consistent winners in these and other mathematics competitions, regularly placing in the top one percent of Canadian math students. Scarborough public schools' students have recently been chosen to represent Canada in the International Mathematics Olympiad, which pits students from countries around the world against tough math questions.

Of course, special education is not only for the gifted; there are thousands of students, from the physically disabled to others with learning disabilities, who must not be ignored. Several years before they were made mandatory by the province of Ontario, the Scarborough board created new curricula and services in this crucial field.

Other programmes deserve acclaim, as well, including the annual Visual Arts Camp, held for up to a week in the woods since the early 1970s. The annual Music Camp, which celebrated its 20th anniversary in 1988, attracts more than 1,300 talented students each June. Scarborough's Bliss Carman Senior Public School exchanges school bands each year with a school in Beech Grove, Indiana. The Scarborough Schools Youth Choir won international awards and toured Britain and Europe under the inspired leadership of conductor Garth Allen. The three business and technical institutes in the city welcome all levels of students to learn occupational and technical skills. The Centre for the Exceptional Athlete, scheduled to open in September 1989, will accommodate students with Olympic games potential, by arranging schedules for athletics and academics. Comments a Scarborough board superintendent, "We give our young exceptional athletes the opportunity to develop their full potential academically and athletically."

Such mastery of the difficult art of educating tens of thousands of students from a large variety of backgrounds did not come easily, nor overnight. And it will be a challenge to continue to provide the same high standards while grants from the province continue to shrink. Still, Scarborough's schools have been leaders among school boards in Canada in computer instruction, right down to the elementary level. And despite the city's relative newness, Scarborough has several schools—West Hill and Agincourt Junior Public schools, to mention just two—which have shot past the quarter-century mark in service to the community.

Scarborough is not immune to the ebb and flow of birth rates, and occasionally schools have closed because of declining enrollment. Yet the city is one of the last in the Metro Toronto area that are still building schools, since houses are still going up, and new communities are being created. "We need this school!" exclaimed the president of the Heathwood Ratepayers' Association when a new elementary school went up in the northwest area of Scarborough in the spring of 1986. "It's nice and bright and very practical," commented its new principal, Rick Graham, about its creative architecture.

The innovations go on in a school board which had a budget in 1987-1988 of over one-third of a billion dollars. And quality education in Scarborough continues long after students reach adulthood. Scarborough enjoys the advantages of two of the country's most impressive post-secondary institutions: the Scarborough campus of the University of Toronto, and Centennial College.

SCARBOROUGH CAMPUS, UNIVERSITY OF TORONTO

Scarborough was uniquely able to provide 300 acres of parkland for a campus of the world-class University of Toronto. Today the Scarborough campus serves over 5,000 students from around the world, most of them Scarborough residents. Students take courses from a faculty of 220 in humanities, life sciences, physical sciences, and social sciences, including some of the most innovative courses in North America, ranging from Canadian studies to "History of Ideas," from "Society, Values, and Medicine" to women's studies. Indeed, its co-operative pro-

Students at Ellesmere Station Public School benefit from the latest in computer instruction. Photo by Dawn Goss/First Light

The Scarborough campus sits amid 300 acres of forest. Courtesy, City of Scarborough

grammes in administration, arts administration, and international development studies are the only ones of their kind offered at the University of Toronto. The earth sciences degree is also extremely strong, and the interdisciplinary degrees in cognitive science and neuroscience are as popular as they are unique.

Unlike the other satellite campus of the university, in Mississauga, the Scarborough campus generated raves, ever since it opened in 1965, and only partly because it was built in its lovely forested ridge and ravine. The massive structure is also architecturally magnificent, with one critic describing it as "not only a building" but "an event." Unarguably, it is. Two large wings, for sciences and humanities respectively, are linked by offices and a meeting area within a four-storey atrium. Even the 33-kilometre drive to the exquisite Scarborough College from the St. George campus in downtown Toronto is pleasant, and there are frequent shuttle buses between the two campuses.

The campus' history begins in 1956, when a committee recommended the establishment of facilities on new campuses as the only alternative to the indefinite enlargement of the downtown campus of the University of Toronto. By 1963, its board of governors purchased the Highland Creek site, at Military Trail and Ellesmere Road, and the sod was turned a year later. In 1965, 191 full-time students were enrolled, taught by 41 members of faculty, using an old biology building on the St. George campus until the magnificent new structure was ready in the first month of 1966.

Like the city in which it stands, the Scarborough campus grew majestically. By 1968, there were 100 members of the faculty, representing 26 disciplines, and by 1970, the college gained increased responsibility for its undergraduate curriculum and independence in its faculty appointments and promotions.

There were but 99 graduates in that first class of 1968; since the early 1980s, between 650 and 700 students graduate each year. Since it opened, over 10,000 young men and women have received BA and BSc degrees from the college.

By the academic year 1974-1975, the enrollment of full-time students exceeded 3,000 for the first time, and has been close to its present capacity ever since. Understandably, over one-third of its students are drawn from Scarborough, and nearly half from other parts of Metropolitan Toronto. But a steady 6 to 8 percent are from other countries.

Scarborough College had achieved such a fine reputation by the early 1970s that it continually had to raise its admission standards. Indeed, what was originally seen as St. George campus' little sister in Scarborough had quickly achieved an identity, character, and attraction of its own. For many years now, the large majority of students offered admission to the University of Toronto have chosen the Scarborough campus as their first choice—even though a great many of them qualify for the main campus.

The 200-plus faculty members now associated with Scarborough College attract over $3 million a year in research grants, and collect many honours, such as the Guggenheim Fellowship of astronomy professor Philipp Kronberg, or the Canada Research Fellowship from the Social Sciences and Humanities Research Council awarded to geography professor Richard Harris. And some 130 Ph.D. candidates and another 50 master's degree candidates are supervised by Scarborough professors, underlining the college's growing maturity on the postgraduate level.

Scarborough College has always sparked innovation. As early as 1975, the college introduced the only formal work-study program in the University of Toronto, and it has stressed a closeness between

This couple enjoys the beautiful surroundings of the Nature Trail at the University of Toronto, Scarborough Campus. Photo by Dawn Goss/ First Light

students and faculty since it first opened its doors.

Scarborough College has a rare spirit, which was shown clearly in the way that students, alumni, faculty, and staff all contributed generously to its library project. The library building, part of the original plan for the college, had been shelved, and the library was housed for years in a temporary space. Its book collection grew from 25,000 volumes to over 175,000, only half of which could be stacked in the library itself. The remaining 87,000 books had to be housed in two bungalows, located nearly half a kilometre away, as well as in storage areas behind kitchens, and in part of a portable classroom.

Students, frustrated by delays in getting books, voted in 1979 to increase their students' fees, and raised nearly $400,000 in just a few years. This extraordinarily constructive initiative was remarkable for many reasons, not the least of which is the fact that improvements would mainly benefit students who would come after them. Eventually, the government and the university joined in support of the project, and a fund-raising campaign was directed to the business community of Scarborough. By 1982, the staff moved to its new, vastly improved location. And today, the younger brothers and sisters of those who fought for a major library on the Scarborough campus have over 200,000 books available on open shelves, as well as maps, periodicals, recordings, and fine arts slides.

Scarborough alumni are to be found around the world, in the ranks of professors, school principals, authors, journalists, editors, dentists, lawyers, physicians, business executives, social workers, industrial scientists, and in the arts and sciences. A 1987 survey of alumni shows that the largest number of graduates are in teaching (19.4 percent of the total responses), with the next two largest groups being accountants and financial employees (10.6 percent) and managers/businesspeople (10.5 percent). A further 7.1 percent are in sales and marketing, 6.3 percent are doctors, dentists, and other medical professionals, and 4.2 percent are engaged in postgraduate study.

From its internationally acclaimed professors to its bicycle paths, nature trails, and even a valley stream, Scarborough College offers unique opportunities. One can rave about its internationally renowned lecturers, including legal giant Thomas Berger and chemistry Nobel Laureate John Polanyi. One can praise the national print exhibition mounted in its art gallery, or the gallery's various shows which reflect the multicultural diversity of Metro Toronto. One can applaud the new soil erosion laboratory, which began construction in the fall of 1988. One can admire the series of Sunday afternoon concerts in its Meeting Place. Or one can take pride in the two straight years that Scarborough College's football team captured the Mulock Cup, the oldest football trophy on the continent. (The college has won the cup four times to date.)

But Scarborough College and its countless successes are best expressed by something that happened in the spring of 1987. Its much-acclaimed humanities programme was selected, among hundreds of other such programmes across North America, as the "ideal model" for a United States federally funded pilot project to renew interest in the humanities. The Foundation for the Improvement of Post-Secondary Education of the U.S. Department of Education looked to Scarborough College to find what it was looking for.

And so have thousands of graduates, who tend to continue living and working in the Scarborough area, where steady growth provides so many opportunities for employment.

Centennial College of Applied Arts and Technology

Every message from the president of Centennial begins with a rather charming declaration, complete with italics: "Centennial College is Ontario's

Centennial College was founded in 1967 to keep up with technology's leaps and bounds. Top photo by Glen Jones. Above photo by Peter Tang/First Light

first college of applied arts and technology."

Centennial has shot up from 514 students attending 14 programmes taught by 29 faculty members in 1966, to over 8,000 students studying in over 70 programmes supervised by nearly 500 teachers today—and on four major campuses. With a present enrollment of another 40,000 part-time students, one can see that Centennial's impact on Scarborough, Metropolitan Toronto, and beyond, has been huge.

Perhaps even more important is the fact that over 95 percent of Centennial's 1987 graduates found employment, and that figure has been consistently over the 90 percent mark for many years, which is precisely what the word "applied" in its name should be all about.

Most colleges of applied arts and technology offer courses in accounting, computer programming, and child care. But Centennial has a surprising number of programmes of a highly original nature: book and magazine publishing; corporate communication; office information administration, the only course of its kind in the province; fibre plastics composites, also unique in the province of Ontario; home furnishings merchandising; and automotive parts merchandising, a course unique to Metro Toronto. Centennial is a college like few others in the world.

The birth of Centennial goes back to the mid-1960s, when the province began to wake up to the fact that our technological society was demanding more specialized education than had been offered up to that time. Prior to World War II, six universities and a handful of nursing schools, teachers' colleges, and agricultural schools were enough. But with the return of the veterans and the explosion of new technology, much more was needed. A number of technical institutes opened in the 1940s and 1950s, offering such subjects as engineering technology, business administration, and technical training.

Then, the public demand for "instant colleges" was so great, that Ontario actually created 19 new colleges in less than 12 months—and we already know which one was the first.

Because 1967 would mark the 100th anniversary of Canada's confederation, the name Centennial was chosen. It set up shop, literally, in a federal building in Scarborough, and the first classrooms were converted from a radar-testing facility. Considering the excellent direction in which the college has always headed, this beginning may have been prescient.

The mandate was straightforward: "To meet the needs of graduates from any secondary school programme, apart from those wishing to attend university, and to meet the educational needs of adults and out-of-school youth, whether or not they are secondary school graduates."

The goal was also clear: to develop high-quality, career-oriented education. Yet in spite of its mammoth enrollment capacity, qualified applicants are turned away every year. There was, and is, a serious need for an institution like Centennial.

From the start, the four main areas of educational programmes have been applied arts, technology, business, and health sciences. The college's curriculum was enriched by the addition of the Toronto East General School of Nursing and Scarborough Regional School of Nursing in 1973, and, 13 years later, the addition of the Nursing Assistant Program of Scarborough General Hospital

Within a half-dozen years of its birth, Centennial began to open other campuses, most of them within the city. The Ashtonbee Campus opened in 1972; it now houses the TIPT, or Transportation and Industrial Power Technology divisions. In that same year, the Continuing Education Division began operating in six satellite campuses, as well as in the two main ones. By 1977, Centennial opened its Progress Campus, the current home of the Engineering Technology and Business Administration divisions. An East York Campus soon followed.

Some facts about Centennial:

*The automotive programmes of the Ashtonbee Campus provide more than four out of five of Ontario's licenced mechanics.

*Centennial was the first college in all of North America to offer full-time robotics programmes.

*A $1.2-million Hospitality Management Centre has been open at its Warden Woods Campus since early 1985, placing over 98 percent of its graduates.

*Centennial has one of the finest alternate-fuel training and development centres on the continent, and is the only Ontario college to offer a program in natural gas conversion.

*The first plastic composites innovation centre in all of Canada opened in late 1985 at its Ashtonbee Campus.

*Centennial is in the forefront of technological computer use, with its CAD/CAM Centre (computer-assisted drafting and design, and computer-assisted manufacturing) at its Progress Campus.

*The college's Management Training Centre offers dozens of vital seminars each fall and spring, on subjects ranging from time management, managing organizational change, customer relations, training the trainer, the Employment Standards Act, and much more.

Centennial College has become a vital part of Scarborough in countless ways, adding to its vitality, as well as its work force. Major speakers, such as Canada's then ambassador to the United Nations, Stephen Lewis, have come to the campus. A new transportation institute, uniting Centennial with the Southern Alberta Institute of Technology (SAIT), provides uniform, Canada-wide standards for the industry. Home day-care provider programmes, unique among Ontario's community colleges, help fill the terrible lack of people qualified to provide home day-care services in Scarborough. The DEL gym at the Progress Campus, considered "the best volleyball, basketball, and badminton facility in Scarborough," according to student life director Chuck Gullickson, is used by community groups and high schools across Metro, and is described as "Centennial's most popular ambassador to the surrounding community." And how could one fail to mention the "Starting a Small Business" course, taught by Frank Miele, the executive director of Scarborough's Economic Development Department? Within a few weeks, fully half the original 40 students began their own businesses.

Centennial College, along with the Scarborough campus of the University of Toronto, follows logically and inevitably from the superb elementary and secondary school system provided by the Scarborough Board of Education. From the latter's fine kindergartens to its early identification of learning abilities, from its French immersion classes to its superior alternative schools and vocational schools, from its programmes for children with special needs to those for the gifted, as well as quality adult education, this city is a place where learning never stops.

CHAPTER SEVEN

A Healthy Look at Hospitals

Like all major and quickly expanding cities in North America, Scarborough has a health department which offers free clinics on family planning and other matters, as well as a nursing division, with its own wide variety of services and programmes. Dental services are available as well, as is advice on nutrition. But long-time residents recall a time when one could not find quality hospital care within the then township's limits.

No longer. In the early 1950s, there was one world-class hospital in Scarborough; by the early 1960s, three; and since 1985, four major facilities. To quote from a headline in the *Scarborough Mirror* in the mid-1980s, "Local Hospitals Prepared Now for Almost Anything." This article went on to say, "The range of services available here means people no longer need to go to hospitals downtown for serious operations like they did years ago." These four impressive institutions are conveniently located right across the large city of Scarborough.

Scarborough General Hospital

In December 1951, when the township of Scarborough was emerging as an attractive alternative to the metropolis to the west, the Sisters of Misericorde decided unanimously to create a new 100-bed hospital. Shortly before construction began, in 1954, Sister St. Roseline, who would be the hospital's first administrator, wrote her impressions of that area of Scarborough. It is difficult to believe that such a description was accurate, less than only four decades ago:

You could reach it, given fair weather, by a dusty, rutted track. In weather not so good, the mud might stop you. When you arrive you would see open fields, with cattle grazing. And there would be a stillness. For this was the country, with city noises far away.

Considering the city surrounding that hospital today, her words are striking. But perhaps more striking is the fact that Scarborough General is today one of the 10 largest community hospitals in all of Canada.

Oliver Crockford was the other major force in the creation of the hospital. In early 1952, he was reeve of the township of Scarborough, and the genius behind the creation of the "Golden Mile of Industry," which marked the real beginning of exponential business growth in the area.

Then, the population of Scarborough was barely 70,000, but when Crockford considered the surrounding municipalities, he recognized the need for a local hospital to serve considerably more than 100,000 people. He met frequently with Sister St. Roseline and the nuns of her order, promising to obtain financial aid not only from senior levels of government, but from the township itself, even though there had been no precedent for such a grant.

The nun and the reeve, helped along by a committee, chose a 25-acre parcel of farmland at the corners of Lawrence Avenue and McCowan Road. It was almost the exact geographical centre of Scarbor-

Scarborough General's emergency department is one of the busiest in the country, with 100,000 people passing through its doors a year. Photo by Glen Jones

Scarborough General owes its existence to the persistence of its first administrator, Sister St. Roseline. Photo by Dawn Goss/First Light

ough, and is today within walking distance from the Scarborough City Hall, Town Centre, Consilium, and downtown; yet at the time, it was far from the centre of population.

The sisters bought the land in July 1952 for $1,200 an acre, which made the total cost a towering $30,000. There were many struggles before Crockford was able to fulfill his promise to the nuns by obtaining a $200,000 grant from the Scarborough Council, but he finally did it. As Sister St. Roseline wrote back then, "At first the public did not want us—they wanted a municipal hospital—and there were many meetings and a real battle. But Mr. Crockford was on our side, and I suspect the good Lord was too. A year after we opened, everyone was in love with us."

Lawrence Avenue was a mere country road, and the sisters were concerned, as the hospital edged toward completion, that there was no way for the healthy, much less the sick, to get there. Finally, Sister St. Roseline phoned the Toronto Transit Commission (TTC) and told them, "Unless you provide buses soon, I'll simply turn the key in the lock and leave."

She also called Oliver Crockford. He had been voted out of the reeveship the previous year, and was no longer an ex-officio member of the hospital board. But Crockford was too involved to quit, so he met with a TTC commissioner, who agreed to drive out to Scarborough to look at the motley street. The commissioner reported back to Crockford that if the road could be improved, he would try to start bus service.

Crockford then talked to a township engineer, who admitted that he still had some spare money in his budget, and would be happy to fix up the road, but it would take time.

Finally, Crockford met with Alan Reavie, a member of the first board at St. Mary's Hospital, and Reavie approached the owner of an automobile dealership of Kennedy Road, who agreed to provide a station wagon and all the gas needed for a jitney service to the hospital. Reavie then went to various firehalls, recruiting enough firemen to act as volunteer drivers. For six weeks, regular trips were made from the corner of Kennedy and Eglinton to the hospital, carrying nurses and other staff who lacked their own cars.

Oliver Crockford became chairman of the board of governors of the hospital in 1963, and held that post until 1972, when the Sisters of Misericorde surrendered ownership of Scarborough General to the government. So it isn't surprising that there is an Oliver E. Crockford

Left: This three-year-old receives personalized speech therapy. Courtesy, Scarborough General Hospital

Below: Scarborough General Hospital offers special tours to broaden the minds of the young. Here, Girl Guides receive a cast demonstration. Courtesy, Scarborough General Hospital

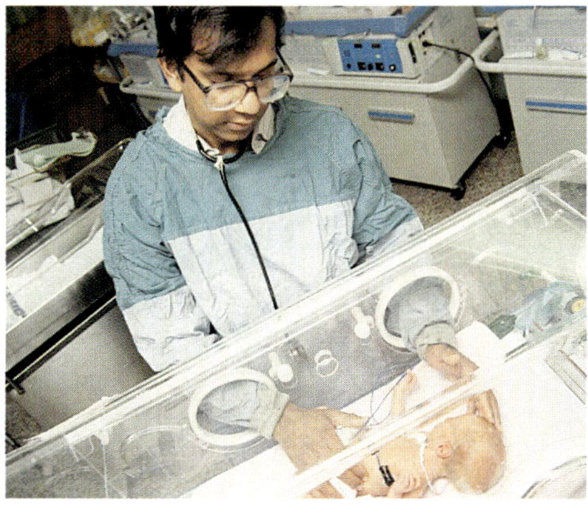

Left: This Pediatrician checks in on a premature newborn in the Special Care Nursery. Courtesy, Scarborough General Hospital

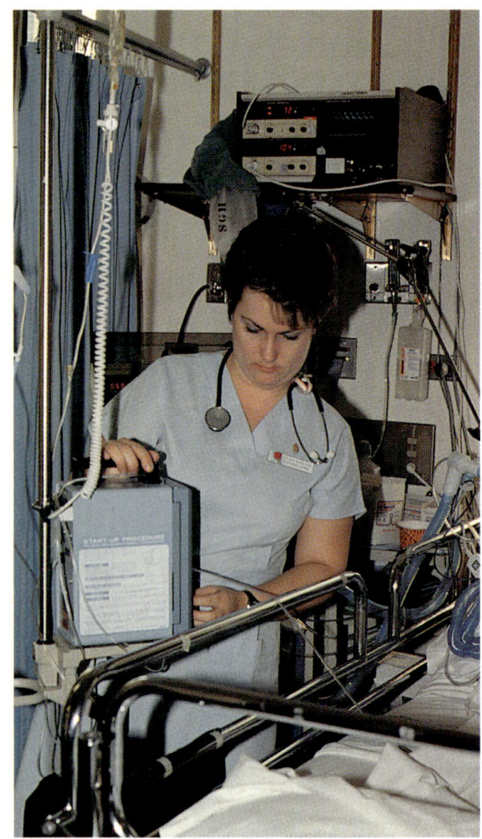

Above: Scarborough General Hospital also offers one-to-one nursing in the Intensive Care Unit. Courtesy, Scarborough General Hospital

Pavilion, a long-term care facility, which opened in 1974. He remained honorary chairman of the General's board of governors until his death in 1985.

Anyone who ever visits bustling Scarborough General Hospital immediately realizes that the hard, steady work of the Sisters of Misericorde and Oliver Crockford was not in vain. Its emergency department is one of the busiest in the country, with more than 100,000 patients passing through its doors each year.

There have been firsts galore. In 1968, the General opened the first burn unit in Canada, and pioneered the use of porcine dressings for burn victims in 1972. Just two years later, it opened the first sports medicine clinic in Metropolitan Toronto, moving many of Canada's finest athletes to take the TTC line to Scarborough for treatment. The General has the largest plastic surgery unit in the country, and with the first surgical laser installed in Scarborough in 1985, the hospital is already renowned in the country for cataract surgery, as well as intraocular lens implants.

After over three decades in operation, there have been many honours for Scarborough General. Dr. Lloyd Carlsen, one of the world's premier plastic surgeons, lectures as far away as Australia, and established the first and only cosmetic surgery hospital in North America. Dr. Harold Stein, a world-renowned and respected ophthalmologist, developed and designed his own lens, and has taught and performed eye surgery in dozens of countries around the world. Dr. Victor Kumar-Misir, after a decade of study, research, and coordination, has received international praise for his multilingual, multimodal communication system, which gathers medical information for doctors and nurses. He is currently working on a system to communicate with the illiterate.

Scarborough General Hospital has become vital to its city, and beyond. Lifeline, a community-based programme, assists the elderly in living independently. They wear a small help button, which, when pressed, automatically dials the Scarborough General Hospital Emergency Response Centre, where trained personnel are available 24 hours a day. The hospital's Speech Pathology and Audiology Department

recently launched Canada's first "Dial a Hearing Screening Test," adding to its value.

After over three decades, Scarborough General Hospital is now a big business, with over 400 medical staff members, and more than 2,000 full- and part-time employees. With 770 beds, over 25,000 patients admitted annually, some 23,000 surgical procedures performed each year, and as one of the country's major centres for microsurgery, the General has proven to be a great success, probably far beyond the wildest dreams and prayers of Oliver Crockford and the Sisters of Misericorde.

Centenary Hospital

The history of Scarborough's Centenary Hospital is briefer than the General's—it opened in 1967, the year that Canada turned 100, but it also took hard work and passionate involvement on the part of many.

If the General had its Crockford, then Centenary had its Margaret Birch. The long-time Member of Provincial Parliament for Scarborough East, and Ontario's first female cabinet minister, Ms. Birch began her long and impressive political career by fighting for a second major hospital in the rapidly growing then borough of Scarborough in the early 1960s. When the hospital opened in Canada's centenary year, she became a founding member of its board of directors, and, in the summer of 1986, she was honoured with the opening of a $30-million Margaret Birch Wing, consisting of four storeys which house a relocated and expanded emergency department, intensive-care unit, and coronary-care unit. The province picked up two-thirds of the tab, Metro Toronto and the city of Scarborough put up another $4 million, and the hospital raised the remainder.

The newspapers of Ontario have been overflowing with news about the quickly expanding hospital over the past few years:

*Its renovated maternity and gynecology unit, featuring a redesigned neonatal intensive-care unit for premature babies with breathing problems.

*Its new mammography service, for early detection of breast cancer.

Facing page, below: Centenary Hospital offers innovative and personal services like the Cuddle Service, where staff members volunteer to cuddle the infants and play with the children in the pediatrics ward. Photo by Glen Jones

Below: Margaret Birch, Ontario's first female Cabinet minister, fought long and hard for the establishment of Scarborough's second hospital. Photo by Dawn Goss/ First Light

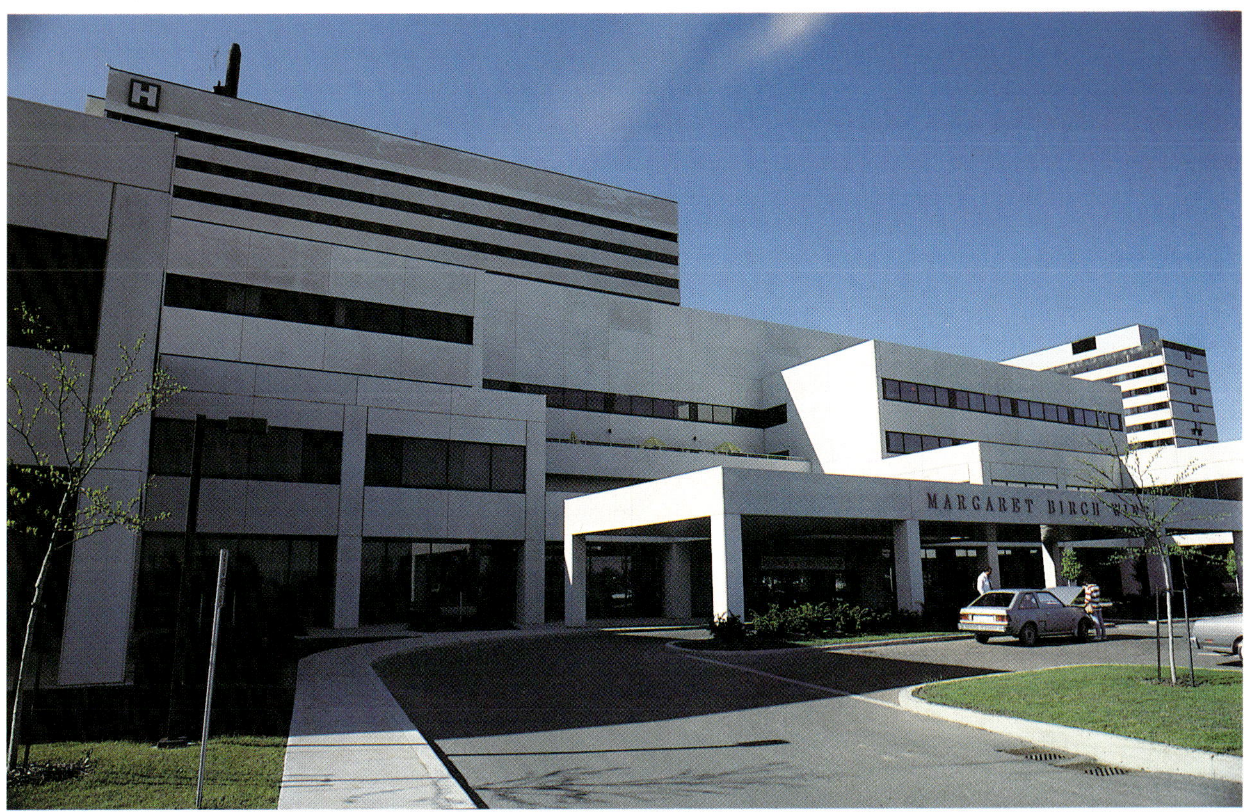

Centenary Hospital's newly acquired CAT Scanner means patients no longer have to travel downtown for specialized tests. Courtesy, Centenary Hospital

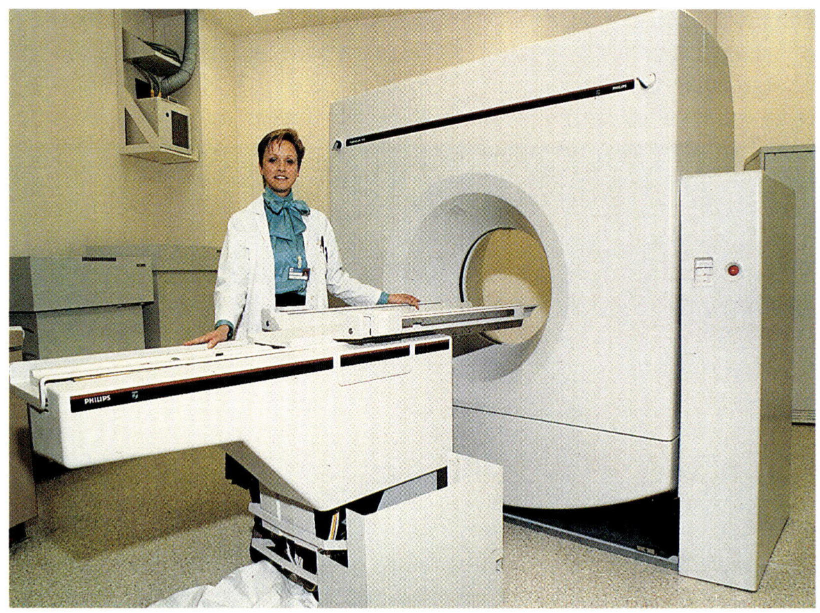

Centenary Hospital was the first community hospital in Ontario with colour doppler equipment used to detect abnormalities of the heart. Courtesy, Centenary Hospital

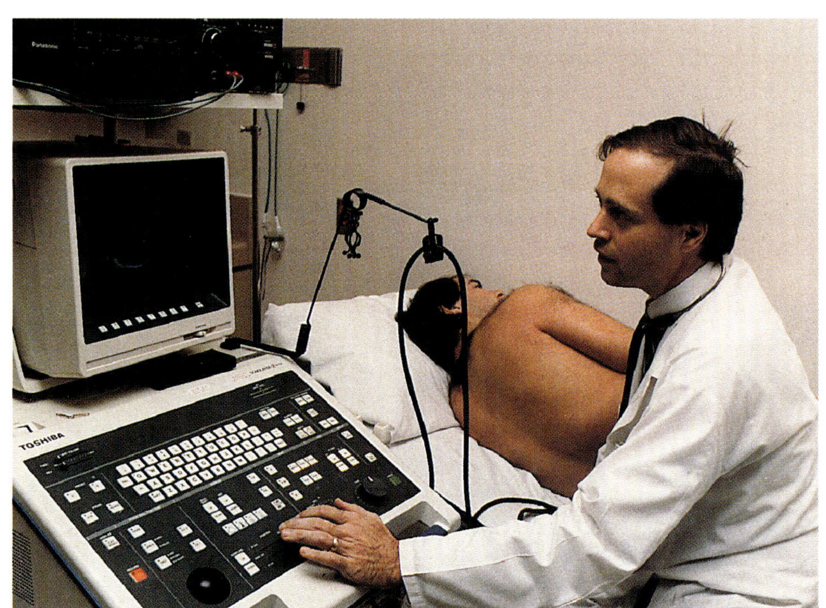

Centenary Hospital's rehabilitation facilities doubled in size during the hospital's expansion. Courtesy, Centenary Hospital

*Its new continuing-care units, providing short-term and long-term reha-
bilitation programmes, chronic care, and respite care for the elderly.

*Its new sports injury clinic, situated in the physiotherapy depart-
ment.

*Its new chiropody service, providing treatment of foot disorders
and basic foot care.

*Its new audiology service, giving Centenary one of the most com-
plete departments dedicated to hearing problems in Metro Toronto.

*Its new, expanded digestive diseases unit, expecting to conduct
over 5,000 treatments by late 1988, rivaling the number of people
served by major downtown Toronto hospitals.

*It's CAT-scanner, housed in the completely renovated diagnostic
imaging (x-ray) department.

*It's ultra-modern diagnostic facilities for heart and lung disease, includ-
ing a cardiac catheterization laboratory.

*It's new Diabetic Centre, offering a comprehensive educational and treat-
ment programme so that hundreds of Scarborough diabetics no longer
have to go to downtown Toronto hospitals for care.

*It's pet therapy programme, providing a permanent canine compan-
ion for geriatric patients.

And so much more. Since Scarborough's Centenary Hospital admitted its first patient in 1967—only four years after it purchased a
26-acre campground from the Boy Scouts—it has grown to 645 beds.
Situated on Ellesmere Road, just a few kilometres east of the City
Centre and less than a mile south of Highway 401, Centenary has
become an essential part of Scarborough, only a little more than two
decades after its creation.

Scarborough Grace Hospital

The "little sister" of health care in the city opened its doors in the fall
of 1985, but had been in the planning stage for many years before. A product of the Salvation Army, it takes its name from the quotation of E.
Stanley Jones: ". . . the first thing in God is love, and grace is love in
action." The new institution is dedicated to doing exactly that—putting
love into action.

In just a few short years, this 302-bed community general hospital
has offered such services as:

*A modern emergency department.

*An intensive-care unit and specially equipped coronary-care unit.

*An obstetrical suite, including birthing, labour, and delivery rooms.

*A rehabilitation and continuing-care unit.

*An in-patient psychiatric unit.

*Out-patient clinics, day surgery, day treatment for seniors, speech
pathology and audiology, physiotherapy, occupational therapy, social
work, and much more.

How much more? Grace is one of the very few hospitals anywhere
to have its own on-site fitness centre, featuring rowing machines, exercise bikes, a complete Global Gym machine, free-weights, and generous
floor space for aerobics classes. Mirrored walls and a stereo system complement the bright and sunny location on the top floor of the hospital.
It is a fine example of a health-care centre encouraging its own staff
members to lead a healthful lifestyle. As the old saying goes, "Physician, heal thyself."

When the Ontario Health Ministry chose to set up two new sexual
assault treatment centres "to provide immediate, compassionate care to victims," it's interesting to note that the then brand-new Scarborough
Grace was one of them.

In July 1987, this crucial centre opened at Grace, and began treating victims who walked in or were brought to the hospital by the police or am-
bulance. Victims of sexual assault are too often put through a "second

*Special care Nursery is offered at
Scarborough Grace Hospital. Courtesy, Scarborough Grace Hospital*

Medical care is offered to young and old alike. Courtesy, Scarborough Grace Hospital

trauma," whether by police or health-care officials, but thanks to this new project at Scarborough Grace, the care team not only assesses and treats the patient, but makes follow-up contact at an appropriate time after the victim's return home. Follow-up care occurs within 72 hours, and a social worker is available to provide counselling. Should the victim wish to press charges, the physician and nurse use a Sexual Assault Evidence Kit from the Centre for Forensic Sciences to gather evidence systematically.

Costing $55 million, four-fifths of which came from provincial and local governments, Scarborough Grace is located at Birchmount and Finch, north of Highway 401. From its cost-effective ambulatory care and out-patient programmes such as laser eye surgery, to its outreach to the multicultural community through an interpreters' service assisting patients in over 40 languages, Grace justly prides itself on being a health-care facility "at the heart of the community." And full of heart, and grace, as well.

Providence Villa

This important member of Scarborough's health-care community since 1962 is often overlooked, and this is ironic when one considers that it has been serving the Metropolitan Toronto area for over 135 years. Providence Villa and Hospital has for much of this time been concerned with the elderly. In its own words, "while most medical institutions are in the business of adding years to life, Providence lays claim to adding life to years."

The earliest origins of Providence Villa can be found in 1648, when the Sisters of St. Joseph were founded in Le Puy, France, to help care for the homeless, the destitute, the orphaned, the sick, and the poor. By the early nineteenth century, the sisters had moved on to the United States, and in 1851, four sisters came to Toronto, and took charge of an orphanage in downtown Toronto. As the needs of that rapidly growing community became more urgent, the sisters' activities expanded as well, gradually embracing teaching, nursing, and caring for the aged. By 1856 the House of Providence was opened on Power Street near Richmond Street.

At its peak, the House of Providence provided accommodation for 700 orphans and elderly residents. But in 1962, the sisters opened a new facility, Providence Villa and Hospital, at 3276 St. Clair Avenue East, in the southern part of the then borough of Scarborough. It was then, as it is now, one of the two major geriatric facilities in the entire Metro area, and was soon serving a population of some 40 percent non-Catholic denominations in its 292 villa beds (residential, extended care, and special care), and 344 hospital beds (chronic care, rehabilitation, palliative, and vacation relief).

But while Providence was continuing its work over the past century for tens of thousands of the elderly and their families, changes in the demographics of both Scarborough and society at large began to demand further changes. The elderly population of Metropolitan Toronto increased by a third over the past decade, and the elderly population of Scarborough and environs is expected to double by the year 2000. The average age of patients at Providence had risen to 85, requiring more care. And a waiting list of over 400 persons meant an up to two-year wait. Action had to be taken.

In 1988, a new, $47-million expansion and upgrading of Providence Villa and Hospital will make it "the state of art in geriatric care," to quote the province's Minister of Health. A $10-million fund-raising drive was begun, and the province promised $20 million of its own toward the eight-year project. On the very first day of that fund-raising campaign, over $5.2 million was raised.

The expansion includes a new home for the aged, containing 290 extended-care beds, and a day-care hospital that will allow people to stay in their homes but receive care at the hospital. In addition, Providence Villa and Hospital has begun to provide services for a number of non-elderly patients.

In less than 40 years, Scarborough has come a long way since a group of nuns had to scrounge for money to create a hospital for the young township. Scarborough has always been a wonderful place in which to be healthy. Since the mid-1950s, it has been a good place in which to be sick, as well.

Another service provided by Scarborough Grace Hospital is Continuing Care for the aged. Courtesy, Scarborough Grace Hospital

Scarborough Mirror
Battle
to put dump
The Mirror
DELIVERY SERVICE

CHAPTER EIGHT

A Very Communicative City

or decades Scarborough has been a communications centre for the entire country. It leads in local television, for one, thanks to Scarborough Television 10. Giant CFTO-TV, which is the flagship of Canada's premier private network, CTV, makes the city a leader in national TV, too. The city has been the home of many of Canada's largest and most influential book publishers for many years, including Prentice-Hall, McGraw-Hill Ryerson, New American Library, and Butterworths. It has two fine local newspapers, the *Scarborough Mirror*, which recently celebrated a quarter-century of serving the people and businesses of Scarborough, and the *Scarborough News*, published by Watson Publishing.

Scarborough Television 10 went on the air in 1969, bringing local programming to what would be a steadily growing clientele. By 1987, Scarborough Cable Communications, its parent company, was providing service to over 90 percent of Scarborough's more than 160,000 homes, and had recently become the first company in Canada to offer full stereo service.

Several years earlier, in 1961, CFTO-TV, also known as Channel 9, began its illustrious career in the Agincourt area of Scarborough, which is today just seconds north of the Scarborough Civic Centre at the northwest corner of McCowan and Highway 401. It would eventually become the most-viewed television station in Canada.

Scarborough Television 10 began broadcasting to its local citizens in 1969 and has steadily provided information to its community. For some 60 hours a week, it offers programming of a surprisingly diverse nature, crowned by "Scarboro Today," a daily news show, which highlights local news, weather, and sports, as well as numerous stories about business developments in the city. And, just as the channel has many firsts, the show has the distinction of being Canada's first daily cable news programme. This is all the more noteworthy since the local newspapers, the *Scarborough Mirror*, *Scarborough News*, and the East Edition of the *Toronto Star* Neighbors supplement are, for all their quality, not daily. In providing daily local news, Scarborough Television 10 provides a great public service.

With merely two studios, a handful of porta-paks and colour cameras, a portable studio at the Civic Centre, and a brand-new mobile production unit, Scarborough Television 10 manages to put on the air such quality programmes as:

*Four and one-half hours of arts and cultural shows each week, including artist interviews, and the show "Arts Scarborough."

*Six hours a week of ethnic programming, such as "Variety of Nations," a half-hour multicultural show which features as many of the 40 different ethnic groups in the city as possible; "Irish Folk," a variety show; and "Stars of Tomorrow," which includes promising artists in performance, and more.

* "Lifestyle," a daily programme which covers everything from financial planning information to profiles of Scarborough's many industries.

* "Strictly Politics," a four-days-a-week show which televises interviews with local, provincial, and federal politicians discussing city

Scarborough Mirror delivery service. Photo by Cliff Spicer

Above: Scarborough Cable Communications recently became the first company in Canada to offer full stereo service. Photo by Jack Holman

Right: The Scarborough Civic Centre is reflected in the windows of Town Centre. Photo by Dawn Goss/First Light

Government services for both Scarborough and the rest of Canada are provided from Canada Centre. Photo by Jack Holman

issues. Episodes on local business, taxes, development, and more are shown.

* "Chat with the Mayor." You guessed it.

It's not easy to cover a rapidly growing, ever-spreading city like this one, especially for a small station like Scarborough Television 10. But its commitment to the community, after two full decades, is both deep and profound. As Cathy O'Brien, spokesperson for the station, declares, "We allow access to the community we serve by giving feedback and participating in both provincial and national cable organizations."

CFTO-TV is its older and much bigger sibling of the airwaves, serving the entire country, as well as Metropolitan Toronto. When CFTO-TV, the flagship of the CTV network, went on the air January 1, 1961, its signal was capable of reaching nearly 3.5 million people. Since that time, the superior programming coming out of its Glen-Warren studios wins kudos across not only Canada, but the entire world.

On its opening day, CFTO-TV became Toronto's only independent television station, as well as North America's most modern television facility. The station has accumulated a solid list of other firsts:

*The first Canadian television station to be fully equipped with colour.

*The first Canadian television station to receive Board of Broadcast approval for full colour transmission, in 1967.

*The first Canadian television station to tape a National Hockey League game in full colour.

*The first Canadian television station to produce a network show in full colour.

*The first Canadian television station to air a colour television programme.

Another first was the 18-hour telethon for the Ontario Association for Retarded Children. It was CFTO-TV's very first broadcast, back in 1961, and it was a milestone in Canadian telecasting. It has been repeated, for dozens of worthy charities, countless times since. A typical, more recent example of the station's largesse was the Children's

Above: Benches and picnic tables line Albert Campbell Square outside the Scarborough Civic Centre. Photo by Dawn Goss/First Light

Miracle Network Telethon for the Hospital for Sick Children Foundation, which ran 24 hours in the last days of May 1987. The hosts of that show included everyone from the wife of Canada's Prime Minister, Mila Mulroney, to CTV's respected national news anchor, Lloyd Robertson, to such talent as opera singer Maureen Forrester, rock genius Ronnie Hawkins, and many more. The Miracle Network Telethon raised over $1.3 million for that charity.

Since the mid-1960s, Glen-Warren Productions Limited has been on the premises of CFTO-TV. Glen-Warren, the production arm of Baton Broadcasting Incorporated, which owns CTV, is one of the largest production companies in the country, and the best videotape facility on the continent, including facilities in New York City and Los Angeles. Its production record is impressive. Its nearly 27,000 square feet of studios, 350 staging and technical crew on staff, 38 state-of-the-art VTR machines, 5 state-of-the-art post-video theatres, and off-line and on-line facilities, have produced Emmy-Award-winning staging design and construction and the largest staging stock in Canada. Many

The Toronto Dominion Data Centre building adds new lines and angles to Scarborough's downtown. Photo by Glen Jones

revered and Emmy-winning television programmes of the past two decades were shot at the CFTO-TV studios in the Agincourt section of Scarborough. Remember "Pygmalion," with Margot Kidder and Peter O'Toole? The hilarious "Pied Piper of Hamelin," part of Shelley Duvall's Faerie Tale Theatre series? Skater Toller Cranston's superb, and award-winning, specials? Many of the Hallmark Hall of Fame shows? Over the last few years, Glen-Warren has also been the shooting address of "All My Sons," "Long Day's Journey into Night," "L.B.J.," "I Would be Called John: Pope John XXIII," as well as handling the editing and post-production work for the highly acclaimed Canadian TV series "Night Heat." Few people are aware that those memorable scenes from the opening of the Academy-Award-winning film *Network*, with Faye Dunaway and Peter Finch, were filmed in Scarborough. He was "mad as hell," and refused to take it anymore in the beautiful and spacious Glen-Warren control booths.

CFTO-TV is the flagship of more than two dozen affiliates of the CTV network because much of its most important national programming originates there, including its excellent morning show, "Canada AM," and its honoured nightly "CTV National News." Because of the former, world leaders from Henry Kissinger to European, Asian, and African prime ministers have headed for the studios in Scarborough. CTV—and dozens of hosts and staff from its flagship station—was the official host of the XV Olympic Winter Games in Calgary in February 1988, providing viewers across Canada and around the world with hundreds of hours of pageantry and excitement.

Even more exciting, for CFTO-TV, Glen-Warren, and Scarborough, was the recent announcement of a new film studio to be built by Glen-Warren Productions Limited. The new sound studio, costing $2.3 million, was built in record time in the spring and summer of 1987, with 14,000 square feet of floor space, and is even larger than CFTO's famed Studio 6, already considered gigantic in the industry.

It means Scarborough's own CFTO-TV will continue to be the centre of television in Canada, while becoming an international film centre, as well. With dozens of American, Canadian, and European films made in the streets of Metro Toronto every year, bringing tens of millions of dollars into its economy, Scarborough has the facilities and communications industry to handle it.

Today, CFTO-TV transmits from the CN Tower, and has a potential viewing audience of some five million people. That represents over one-fourth of all the households in Canada, and two-thirds of the households in the province of Ontario. This figure doesn't even include the additional millions across Canada who watch its Scarborough-made programming on CTV affiliate stations.

Not all of the world's communications are done electronically, of course. The history of Scarborough's "mirror" on the news is relevant here, as well, since that fine local newspaper has prided itself for a quarter-century on its ability to inform the city's citizens about the events affecting them close to home.

The origins of the *Scarborough Mirror* go back over three decades, to the time when a group of determined individuals formed the Metro Mirror Publishing Company in an eastern Toronto warehouse. But even earlier, the concept of a community newspaper for Scarborough burned in the heart of then 29-year-old Russ Eastcott, a broadcaster who lived in nearby Don Mills. After doing some volunteer publicity work for a local councillor, he recognized the potential for a community publication, and began to approach businesspeople in the Scarborough area. The responses were universally enthusiastic. Toronto's three major papers too often ignored the prosperous, booming borough of Scarborough.

At the same time, in Vancouver, a 21-year-old graduate of Toronto's Ryerson Polytechnical Institute named Ken Larone was writing for the *Vancouver Sun*. He, too, became intrigued with the idea of publishing a community newspaper in his home town, having been impressed by the successes of similar projects in the United States.

The first opportunity arose in Coldwater, Ontario, where Andrew MacLean, of the MacLean publishing family, started a newspaper called the *Canadian*. Larone moved east and became its editor. It didn't last long there, but they decided to revive the paper in the small but quickly expanding community of Don Mills, on the western edge of Scarborough.

It was then 1956, and both Russ Eastcott and Andrew MacLean were working independently to fulfill their respective, related dreams of a newspaper of the eastern portion of Metro Toronto. Only three weeks before the publication of the first issue, each man learned of the other's work.

There was already a small local paper called *Don Mills News*, and the new entrepreneurs realized that the community could hardly support three newspapers. So Eastcott joined forces with MacLean and Larone, and the *Don Mills Canadian* first hit the streets on January 17, 1957.

Personality conflicts soon arose, along with arguments over the editorial content of the fledgling paper. MacLean found himself the odd man out, and the paper quickly ceased publication. Larone and Eastcott wouldn't quit, though, and they formed Metro Mirror Publishing Company, borrowing the huge sum of $2,000 from some friends to make it happen, and within a few days, the *Don Mills Mirror* was rolling off the press.

It was a lively tabloid, overflowing with pictures of babies, schoolchildren, and families, as well as countless stories about community affairs, events, and businesses. It was a success with advertisers, and soon thrived. Within a few years, Metro Mirror was producing a second paper, the *York Mills Mirror,* serving that northern suburb of Metro. It wasn't long before the men turned their attention to Scarborough, the very attractive borough taking off just a few miles to the east.

All this expansion demanded more money, leading to the sale of one-half of the firm to the Torstar Corporation, the giant publisher of the *Toronto Star.* Larone and Eastcott now had the capital necessary to expand into Scarborough, and Torstar benefitted from a large interest in a newspaper that would serve as a flagship for a planned chain of suburban publications.

On May 3, 1962, the first issue of the *Scarborough Mirror* came out of a small plaza near Victoria Park Avenue, and it was an instant success. "There was such a high level of community interest and burgeoning growth within the community," recalls Russ Eastcott. "Scarborough was a great place to have a newspaper. I think more than anything, we were pleased to be part of a new phenomenon of suburban living."

By 1972, after creating further suburban papers, both Eastcott and Larone moved on, having sold their remaining one-half interest to Torstar. Since 1981, the *Scarborough Mirror* has been part of a chain of over a dozen community newspapers across southern Ontario known as Metroland Printing, Publishing and Distributing.

By 1983, the *Mirror* was delivered free to over 50,000 households in the city; by 1984, it had moved to larger offices near Markham and Finch, and was joined by a 63,000-square-foot printing plant. Just three years later, Metroland more than doubled the size of its printing facilities in Scarborough.

In April 1986, the *Scarborough Mirror* expanded to twice-weekly publication, and it continues to thrive as one of the finest community newspapers in the country, winning dozens of national, as well as provincial, awards for editorial and advertising excellence. "We've come a long way in 25 years and we're hoping to go a lot further in the years ahead," exclaims the *Mirror*'s present publisher, Ken Koyama, who has also been publishing an important business monthly since 1986, the *Business Leader.*

Whether due to the fine local programming of Scarborough Television 10 or the equally fine local reporting of the *Mirror,* whether from the world-class Canadian publishing companies which call Scarborough home, or the world-class facilities and programming of CFTO-TV, this city reaps the benefit of thousands of jobs and tens of millions of dollars in salaries and advertising.

This is the busy newsroom of the Scarborough Mirror. *Photo by Cliff Spicer*

CHAPTER NINE

A Superior Transportation Network

carborough is located in the very heart of southern Ontario, the most prosperous area in all of Canada. Indeed, the city is closer to the bulk of the U.S. market, which happens to be in its northeast, than are California, Texas, and Florida. With approximately four-fifths of Canadian exports entering the U.S. duty-free in the 1980s, it is a terrific advantage for manufacturers situated in Scarborough to be so close to American, as well as Canadian, markets.

The city offers the hundreds of new businesses settling in Scarborough all the advantages of a major North American urban centre, but at vastly lower cost than competing downtown areas in Boston, New York City, Buffalo, or even Toronto.

Smart businesspeople know full well that they must be able to get products and people to and from an area to make it truly worthwhile.

Scarborough comes through, due to its superb location, but even more, thanks to its remarkable growth, which has moved the federal, provincial, and municipal governments to build even better transportation facilities to and from the city.

Pearson International Airport is just west of Scarborough. It was recently named after the late Canadian prime minister and Nobel Peace Prize winner Lester B. Pearson. One of the world's major airports, it offers far more than 1,200 domestic and overseas flights every day. Nearly every major and minor airline in the world today serves the two bustling terminals of Pearson, and with a third terminal being built in 1988, the facility will continue to grow in both importance and reliability.

The most frequently flown route in all of Canada is between Toronto's Pearson and Montreal, on which Air Canada alone runs 28 flights daily. Add 17 more trips each way on Canadian Airlines International, and 3 more on Wardair, and you get a sense of just how busy the airways are between just those two cities. There is also frequent service to both coasts, and Air Canada, to choose but one example, offers three non-stops daily to Chicago, and a full dozen a day to New York. In a nutshell, getting in and out of the Toronto area to and from almost any major airport in North America is no more difficult than flying from, say, Chicago to Denver, or Dallas to Washington, D.C.

Connections are frequent and good, both coming and going, and although the majority of air passengers are on business, a solid portion of each flight is filled with tourists and visitors.

Although tiny by comparison, the two regional airports near Scarborough are also worth mention, since they provide handy local services to add to those of Pearson. Buttonville Airport, just a few minutes north of Scarborough, serves military and private aircraft only, but has been a boon to many a business traveller over the years. Down on the waterfront is the tiny but very handy Toronto Island Airport, from which short-takeoff-and-landing de Havilland Dash 7 and Dash 8

The Macdonald-Cartier Highway stretches from Windsor to Montreal, spanning as many as 16 lanes as it crosses metro Toronto. Photo by Peter Tang/First Light

planes make regular flights to and from such major Canadian cities as Montreal, Ottawa, and London, as well as Newark, Rochester, and Buffalo. Between Pearson International Airport and these two smaller airports it is easy for anyone to get to and from Scarborough without delay.

On the ground, the two major railroads of Canada, Canadian National and Canadian Pacific, provide service through the city along one of the finest spur line networks in the entire area of Metropolitan Toronto. Whether filled with passengers from Montreal and points east or auto parts on the way to Vancouver, CP and CN are among the most reliable railway companies anywhere.

Furthermore, once every day, an Amtrak passenger train arrives from New York City, via Buffalo, and another comes from Chicago, through Detroit and Windsor. Each pulls into Union Station, near Lake Ontario, less than a half-hour from the Scarborough City Centre.

Not far from the heart of Scarborough are the custom's docking facilities of Oshawa, to the east, and the huge Toronto Harbour, to the southwest. Both are just minutes away, providing manufacturers with further reliable choices for movement of their products to other parts of North America, even Europe, Africa, and Asia. While the city of Scarborough itself is not a shipping point, its proximity to both of these docks can be invaluable for both manufacturing and warehousing in the area.

Also impressive in the world of transportation is the absolutely superb highway system of southwestern Ontario, which cuts through Scarborough like nerves in a very healthy body. There are three major highways in and out of the city, the most important being the Macdonald-Cartier Expressway, known better across Metro Toronto and all of Canada as Highway 401.

Stretching proudly from Windsor, Ontario, in the southwest, to Montreal, Quebec, in the northeast, the 401 is a remarkably well-kept, yet toll-free highway, reaching an expanse of up to 16 lanes as it makes its way across the northern portion of Metropolitan Toronto, from Pearson Airport on its western edge to Scarborough's own Metro Zoo on the east.

The 401 was thoughtfully built, with carefully planned collector and through lanes, making Scarborough only a single day's drive from over 120 million potential customers across North America.

Furthermore, a 1,200-kilometre network of high-capacity, well-maintained local roads through Scarborough, and the neighbouring Don Valley Parkway, called Highway 404 when it moves north of the 401, allow one to drive people or truck products to the booming north of the city or to downtown Toronto in a matter of minutes.

An electronically controlled highway will soon extend across Highway 401, from Highway 427 all the way to Neilson Road near the Metro Zoo. The plan, called the Freeway Traffic Management System (FTMS), will cost well over $20 million, and will include television cameras, underground vehicle detectors, and computerized traffic warning signs.

Television cameras on 15-metre poles will be placed 500 metres apart along either side of the highway, each camera "seeing" for one kilometre, allowing a visual overlap of 500 metres each. The closed-circuit television system will enable FTMS employees to dispatch police immediately, as well as warn motorists of traffic hazards from a central monitoring system. From there, technicians will send signals to the message signs on the highway, such as "ACCIDENT AHEAD—LEFT LANE CLOSED." They will also be able to notify police, other emergency assistance, and radio stations.

Waiting for citizens to phone in traffic accidents, or for aerial helicopters to spot them, can mean a 15- to 20-minute delay in getting help to the scene. With FTMS, highway accidents across the top of Metro Toronto should decrease by as much as 20 percent by the early 1990s, and enable rush-hour traffic to move close to 50 percent faster than usual. The system will also minimize energy consumption, since those traffic jams can burn a lot of gas, and improve both safety and use of highways. Metro Toronto is one of the few places in Canada where this new technology is being used.

The much-celebrated Rapid Transit (RT) line connects Scarborough Civic Centre to downtown Toronto, and to the rest of the superb Toronto Transit Commission (TTC) trolley and bus services, serving nearly every part of Metro Toronto. RT is one of the most extraordinary aspects of Scarborough's transportation system. For a booming city like Scarborough, which attracts so many tens of thousands of employees who live elsewhere in the area, the RT is both a boon and a blessing.

On the day the Scarborough RT line made its debut, on March 22, 1985, the quotes from the big-wigs flew hot and heavy:

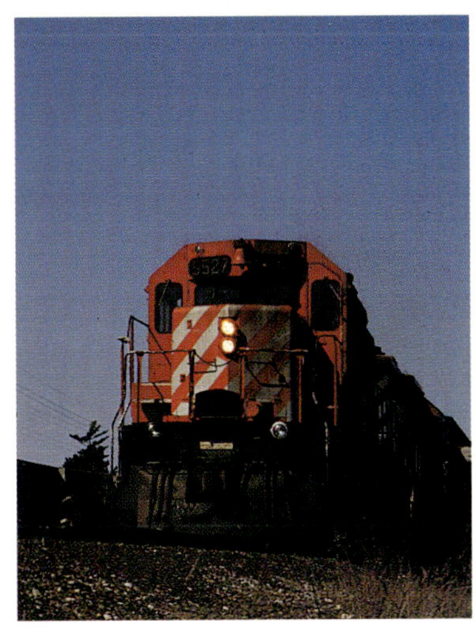

Above: Canadian Pacific provides passenger service along one of the finest spurline networks in metro Toronto. Photo by Glen Jones

Top: The Via (CN) Rail travels throughout the metropolitan area. Photo by Glen Jones

Above: The RT whisks riders from downtown Scarborough to the heart of Toronto in less than half an hour. Courtesy, City of Scarborough

Above right: Scarborough's RT is the cutting edge of transportation technology. Courtesy, City of Scarborough

Scarborough's Rapid Transit line connects with the Toronto Transit Commission, serving all parts of Metro Toronto. Photo by First Light/ Lorraine C. Parrow

The RT line passes through downtown Scarborough and by the Prudential buildings. Photo by Glen Jones

* "The RT is proof positive that Ontario can challenge the world and produce the best facilities anywhere," was the message from the then premier of the province, Frank Miller.

* "The TTC is proud to showcase the exciting new technology and move into the computer age," said the commission's chairman.

* "This is the greatest day in the history of Scarborough," rejoiced Mayor Gus Harris.

None of them was exaggerating. For the RT was, in fact, the first computerized, intermediate-capacity urban transit system to enter revenue service in all of North America, and irrefutably the most advanced system on the continent.

The RT was built at a cost of $196 million, and its raison d'être was to link the civic and commercial hub of Scarborough with the eastern terminus of the Bloor-Danforth subway line. One could now get from the heart of downtown Toronto to the heart of downtown Scarborough in less than half an hour.

A boon, and a tremendous boom to Scarborough, as well. For, apart from its extremely impressive technical sophistication, the high-tech system plays a mammoth role in transforming Scarborough from a rural suburb to a truly great city in its own right.

Work began on the Scarborough RT project in October 1981. Between that year and the summer of 1987, over $2.6-billion worth of building permits were issued by the city of Scarborough. In fact, during the year that the RT began its service, the city of Scarborough saw developments worth half a billion dollars in the area of the City Centre.

The Scarborough RT was the product of over five years of intensive engineering, design, and construction work, and its advanced technology, created in Ontario, incorporated three significant innovations:

*Computerized train operation for safety, reliability, and efficiency;

*Linear induction motors for improved all-season performance without pollution—and with no moving parts;

*Steerable-axle trucks for quiet, smooth rides and reduced maintenance costs.

The RT's computers control the vehicle speeds, maintaining safe distances between trains. Yet the TTC chose to retain an operator on board to control station stop times and door operation, and to verify that the track is clear before leaving each station.

All that, and two- to six-car trains cruising along at 45 miles per hour at 2.5 to 4-minute intervals, allowing very little time for cursing when one misses the train.

The Rapid Transit (RT) line's Civic Centre station awaits passengers. Photo by Glen Jones

The ridership on the RT nearly doubled in the first two years after it opened its doors to the eager public. In its first year of operation, there were but 19,000 passengers taking the RT each day; as of the summer of 1987, that number was up to 35,000 every single day. With an ultimate capacity of 20,000 passengers per hour, per direction, there is little fear of overcrowding, in spite of Scarborough's impressive, and continuing, growth.

The TTC completed a two-year winterization programme in 1987 to improve the RT's reliability. Under this $1.5-million programme, heating cables, power rail coverboards, and track switch heaters were installed to counteract the effects of icing and freezing rain on the electrically powered line.

"The Scarborough RT strongly encouraged office development in the City Centre area," says Steve Warbuck, the director of commercial projects for a property management firm. Adds Jay Cross, the general manager of Prudential Insurance's real estate operations, "There's no question that the rapid transit link is a positive factor when corporations consider relocation. It helps to make an office relocation of personnel to Scarborough a smooth one."

Now the question arises, just what is Scarborough making that has to get in and out of the city so rapidly and at such little cost? A glance at some recent numbers from the City's Economic Development Department will give some idea of just how much there is:

*During the decade between 1971 and 1981, the entire province of Ontario grew 2.5 percent each year in manufacturing. During the same period, Scarborough averaged 5.4 percent annual growth.

*During that same decade, the province grew 4.3 percent in transportation industries. In Scarborough, the average was 8.2 percent.

*In trade the province grew 4.6 percent, while Scarborough grew 7.5 percent.

Census of Manufacturers of Statistics Canada in Ottawa figures tell the story of manufacturers in Scarborough, between 1976 and 1981:

*Food and beverages: in 1976, manufacturers numbered 38, with 2,538 employees; by 1981, the number was up to 47, with 3,492 employees. The percentage increase in each category was 23.7 and 37.6, respectively.

*Rubber and plastics: from 33 businesses employing 1,311, to 47 employing 2,041, for a change of 42.4 percent and 55.7 percent, respectively.

*Furniture and fixtures: 38 companies with 792 workers in 1976, to 49 companies and 976 workers in 1981, for a change of 28.9 percent and 23.2 percent.

*Paper and allied industries: 28 establishments with 2,375 employees in 1976, becoming 35 establishments with 3,121 employees in 1981, for increases of 25.0 percent and 31.4.

*Printing and publishing: from 86 businesses and 1,968 employees, up to 124 businesses and 2,856 employees, growing 44.2 percent and 45.1 percent.

*Electrical products: 59 companies with 5,742 workers, becoming 73 with 6,354, growing 23.7 percent and 10.7 percent.

*Transportation equipment: 26 manufacturers with some 3,318 employees, to 43 companies, with 3,945 employees, for an increase of 65.4 percent and 18.9 percent.

A more recent collection of data, from the city's director of economic research, Arie Ashkenazy, compares manufacturing and warehousing in Scarborough over 1985-1986 to the other cities which comprise Metropolitan Toronto, and shows that Scarborough grew 6.1 percent while its neighbouring cities grew 3.4 percent, 2.8 percent, 1.1 percent and even lost up to 5.6 percent of their jobs in those categories.

Scarborough has become a hotbed of manufacturing and warehousing, at least partly because of the availability of good transportation.

The Canadian Pacific Railroad is among the most reliable railway companies in the country. Courtesy, City of Scarborough

CHAPTER TEN

A United Nations of Ethnicity

few years ago on Newspaper Carrier Day, the twice-weekly local paper, the *Scarborough Mirror*, honoured its delivery kids by listing their names in a full page. No amount of description of Scarborough's cultural and ethnic vibrancy can capture what this list of a few hundred children could.

Here are just a handful of the carriers' names;

Michael Assiviero	Robert Schmelefske
Krista Vandermeer	Dennis Villagomez
Vasant Moro	Bobby Sengsiry
Danny Demedeiros	Chahe Tombazian
Arun Balakrishnan	Kyle Dubeau
Sharon Herbert	Michael Iacolucci
Maureen McBryan	Jimmy Hristov
Shawn O'Sullivan	Bartek Smolczynski
Sameer Punja	James Kim
Lau Hau	Inchun Moon
Mark Chung	Paul Singh

For countless reasons, ranging from more reasonable housing to always-increasing employment opportunities, Scarborough has become one of the most exciting ethnic and cultural mixes in Metropolitan Toronto, in Canada, even in the world. More importantly, this increased diversity has meant a richer life for everyone, socially, economically, and spiritually.

Not so long ago, Scarborough was a farming community, with houses and barns as solid and hardy as the British, Scottish, German, and American men and women who came to Canada to build them. But the years since the Second World War have profoundly enriched this country and city with newcomers—many of whom helped put Scarborough on the world map.

According to the 1981 census figures, nearly one-half of Scarborough's residents claim ethnic origins other than British.

But who needs a census? Here are just a few recent headlines, along with a bit of each story, from recent issues of the *Mirror:*

*Sikh Temple Will Be Built: City council approved the construction of a Sikh temple across the road from a Hindu temple Monday by a vote of 15 to 4 . . . (November 5, 1986)

*Chilean Family Flees to Canadian Safety: Mario Arevalo was arrested in Santiago, Chile last year. His crime—giving medical supplies to a church-run clinic . . . In early February, Arevalo, his wife, Felicita, who is seven months' pregnant, and his two sons, Alexis, 11, and Leandro, 4, arrived in Canada as refugees . . . The Arevalos are typical of the 15 refugee families that come to Scarborough each month . . . (April 4, 1987)

*Chinese Pay TV Hits Scarborough: The man responsible for the world's first Chinese pay television has big plans for Scarborough. Francis Cheung, who came to Canada four years ago with his family . . .

St. Anne Ukranian Church contributes these picturesque steeples to Scarborough's skyline. Photo by Glen Jones

Above: Ethnic dancers entertain at the Metro Toronto Zoo. Photo by Lorrain C. Parrow/First Lighte

Top: Folk dancing is one of the many activities conducted at the Civic Centre. Courtesy, City of Scarborough

Right: Especially since World War II, immigrants have made Scarborough their home. Courtesy, City of Scarborough

incorporated Chinavision Canada Corporation in July 1983 and last spring won a controversial Canadian Radio-television and Telecommunications decision for a pay-TV licence . . .

As an astute businessman who has rarely been wrong in the past, Cheung says Scarborough is one of his favourite marketing areas within the Metro region. "From the viewpoint of the Chinese, Scarborough is regarded as a new, developing area with a big future. It's becoming very active. The business will grow rapidly . . ." (September 5, 1984)

The exciting influx of new Canadians has made itself obvious in business, in the arts, in industry, in service, and in education. Often using 1981 census figures, but not always, let's take a brief tour—and a very incomplete one, understandably, since the city is growing all the time—of Scarborough's ever-growing ethnic communities!

East Indians

There are some 40,000 East Indians in Scarborough, who have already set up a large network of organizations and clubs, many of them religious, and most of them meeting in private homes. Yet for a special event, such as the Indian New Year, Dewali, over 750 annually pack a high school auditorium.

Each winter, the Hindu Cultural Society celebrates the Maha Shivratri celebration and Lord Shiva's consecration at their temple on Ellesmere Road in the city. The stunning celebration marks the symbolic marriage of two parts of God—Shiva, or the father aspect, and Ratri, or the mother aspect.

"The Indians are a very warm, hospitable people," declares Aruna Koushik, of the Indian Immigrant Aid Services, and it appears Scarborough has returned that warmth and hospitality.

Above: Dressed in customary attire, these women head to a gathering at the Hindu Cultural Society. Photo by Dawn Goss/First Light

Below: At the Zoodo, a Metro Toronto Zoo event, this firebreather captivates the crowd. Photo by Lorraine C. Parrow/First Light

The St. Nicholas Greek Orthodox Church features this ornate, gilded interior. Photo by Peter Tang/First Light

Greeks

Over 15,000 Greeks were listed as living in Scarborough in the 1981 census. They have thrived in business, and on any Sunday, one can find a healthy number of the city's Greeks at the St. Nicholas Greek Orthodox Church on Finch Avenue, practicing their ancient and revered faith, and at the St. John Community and Youth Centre on Warden Avenue.

A passion for politics is so strong in the Greek community that a member of Parliament was recently urged by his supporters to print his newsletters in Greek, as well as English, so recent immigrants to Scarborough could better follow his activities. It did not take long to convince the politician to do so.

West Indians

By the 1981 census, close to 30,000 natives of the Caribbean had come to the geographically colder but entrepreneurially warmer city of Scarborough. Many of the immigrants were business and professional people who chose to escape the failing economies and unstable political circumstances in a number of the islands of the West Indies. It's been a brain drain on their homelands, but a most promising influence upon Scarborough.

There are local organizations like Tropicana, Caribbean Chinese Association, and a YWCA programme called "Focus on Change" for West Indian women, and the future looks good for this dynamic minority.

As West Indian spokespersons have noted, the many immigrants from the Caribbean fit easily into Canadian society, because most are well-educated, have something to offer their chosen homeland, and have similar values. One man from Jamaica even got a street named after him: Ben Johnson Drive, in a new subdivision.

He was honoured for shattering the world record for 100 metres in Rome in the summer of 1987, winning the first gold medal for Canada at a world championship since Duncan McNaughton won the high jump at the 1983 Olympics. Before 64,500 in the stadium, and millions more watching on television around the world, the 25-year-old native of Falmouth, Jamaica, left quadruple Olympic gold-medalist Carl Lewis of the United States behind him. Johnson's 9.83 seconds made him the fastest man in the world, and Scarborough was fast to claim him as one of their own. "He trained with the Scarborough Optimists Track Club, he represented Scarborough at the Peace Games, he was raised in Scarborough and lives there," said a proud city alderman at the time. Although it wasn't the only way for a Caribbean native to be honoured in Scarborough, it sure was a quick way. Just 9.83 seconds, in fact.

Chinese

Unlike most other ethnic groups in Scarborough, whose businesses and after-work pleasures are spread across the city, the Chinese community tends to concentrate both its resources and its commercial involvement between Finch on the south, Steeles on the north, Victoria Park on the west, and Brimley on the east.

Fully half of Scarborough's Chinese live north of Sheppard Avenue, and their most colourful shops can be found in the East Court Mall, and the very successful Dragon Centre. And where else, outside of the Far East, can one encounter papier-mâché lions dancing away evil spirits, or scenes performed from a Chinese opera?

More than a quarter of the Chinese population is employed in the professions in Scarborough. They are found frequently in education, law, medicine, and architecture. Many are immigrants from Hong Kong, anxious to leave that city before the British lease is up near the end of this century.

One can wander into the Tai Cheong Supermarket in the Dragon Centre, and purchase some fried fish paste, or Wu Chung white jelly fungus, or Koon Yick Wah Kee chili and garlic sauce, not to mention Chinese tea in a lovely pink tin covered with Oriental figures, water chestnut starch, shark's fin cake, dried lotus seeds, squid, mussels, and much more.

Or one can visit the Agincourt Garden Bakery in the East Court Plaza, and enjoy some of the joys of the oven of husband-and-wife team Stephen and Shelley Chow: delicious black bean cake, filled to overflowing with bean paste, black bean balls, deep-fried with sesame seeds on top and bean paste inside, and melon cakes, made with a fine, flaky pastry and filled with astonishingly sweet melon. And why not some barbecued pork pies to take along to the zoo for a picnic?

One can pick up over four dozen magazines in Chinese at Sun Wah Bookstore in the Dragon Centre, or some Pearl Powder at Shou Er Kang Chinese Herbs Ltd., which is recommended for such ailments as "fever, insomnia and decline of organs." Should one run short of cash, there's always the Hong Kong Bank of Canada just a few steps away, designed to look exactly like the original one back home in China.

There are dozens of other nationalities and cultures in Scarborough, literally too numerous to mention. Some of these citizens have helped publicize the city far beyond its own borders. For instance, two major Scarborough citizens of German descent:

Horst Kroll, who operated his own auto service business in Scarbor-

Diners flock to Hsin Kuang Restaurant on Finch Avenue. Photo by Glen Jones

The colorful altar at St. Peter and Paul Ukranian Catholic Church soars to the high ceiling. Photo by Peter Tang/First Light

ough for nearly two decades, is one of Canada's top road-racing drivers, and has been at it professionally for a full quarter-century, racing throughout Canada, the U.S., and Europe in cars he designs and constructs. He captured the Canadian Championship twice, was named Canadian Driver of the Year twice, and holds three National Formula Vee titles. In fact, he recently raced in the Can-Am in Los Angeles, in a car painted in the Scarborough colours of blue, gold, and white and displaying its motto, "City of the Future, Scarborough, Ontario, Canada." "I'm proud to live here and I'm doubly proud now that I'll be racing for Scarborough," Kroll said at the time.

Monika Schnarre is another Scarborough resident of German extraction. She was chosen the world's top model in Hollywood, California, in January 1986. The straight-A student at Woburn Collegiate Institute in Scarborough was chosen "Supermodel of the World" after beating dozens of contestants from 26 countries in a nationally televised contest. The win brought the brown-haired, blue-eyed teenager up to $250,000 in modelling contracts from the famed Ford Agency in New York, and she has since appeared on the covers of such major Canadian magazines as *Flare* and *Chatelaine,* and even the internationally read *Vogue* and *Sports Illustrated.*

A chapter on ethnicity should not ignore someone like Anita Scott, known as the Queen of Scarborough. She has lived in the city since 1959, when she emigrated from London, England. Scott is Scarborough's only Pearly Queen, which is a type of English pub entertainer in an outrageous costume, a tradition going back to the 1890s, when various women would sing and collect for money in east-end London. Anita Scott is a professional, yet she somehow manages to squeeze four to five dozen benefit shows into her schedule every year; "a labour of love," she calls them. From nursing homes to the Cancer Society's annual parade, Scott continues to spread joy across Scarborough and all of Canada. "It's a good feeling when a smile breaks out. That's something you can't buy," she declares.

Scarborough has truly become a kind of United Nations North, where tens of thousands of recent immigrants from Europe, Asia, Africa, and most every country one can think of, seem to get along a lot better than their original country's representatives do, down south at the U.N. It hasn't been all roses, of course; most of these ethnic groups and their members have struggled hard to make it in Scarborough, to find their place in the business and social communities, while maintaining the languages, cultures, religions, and values of their native countries.

It was not the Scarborough Bluffs which attracted so many of Canada's new immigrants to the city. As a local magazine noted, earlier this decade: "Economic factors play a large part in the establishment of any community, and the Chinese community is no exception. [In 1984] land in Scarborough cost about $20 per square foot, making the cost to developers approximately one-tenth of those in the Spadina area of Toronto [older Chinatown] where the cost is $200 per square foot . . . The attraction to Scarborough is obvious." The numbers have changed, but not the advantages.

Delis, restaurants, and bakeries to suit a variety of tastes are in Scarborough. Photo by Jack Holman

Local residents eat at Santos Place. Photo by Jack Holman

CHAPTER ELEVEN

The Scarborough Civic Centre

carborough's municipal government was named one of the top 50 in all of North America in the fall of 1986. The city was picked because of its impressive computerized resource management programme, developed by its Works Department. The programme keeps track of roads, sidewalks, traffic lights, and all other works projects, and issues repair orders when needed.

It works like this: if a citizen encounters a problem relating to any public works activity, he or she simply phones a single Works Department number exclusively for problems of that kind. Three full-time clerks take down the information (there is a 24-hours-a-day line as well, for major emergencies only), and then feed it directly into a computer. Depending on the importance of the situation—a sewer back-up could have work crews on the scene in less than half an hour—orders are produced immediately, on-line, and the assignment is issued. A missing sign, a pothole, or a broken sidewalk might not be repaired for a day or longer, of course. Still, it is interesting to note that at the time Scarborough won its award, the work orders were sent out overnight. Today, they can be instantaneous.

There were over 1,000 towns and cities across Canada and the United States that were observed, but in order to be chosen for the honour, "the winning cities must have shown innovation in solving problems as well as be willing to share it with other municipalities," said a spokesperson for the New York-based network which gives out the awards. "And that certainly describes Scarborough."

This single award helps illustrate that particular intelligence and creativity in planning, also shown in the thoughtful, careful development of the heart of the city's downtown, that has been reflected in its municipal success. It has not hurt the city to be a fairly late-blooming, until only recently rural community. Look around at other world-class cities, and one sees downtowns that are more often than not chaotic, confused, and meandering. Scarborough deserves all the credit for its forward-looking planning, and it is receiving that credit, too.

One might well begin with the attractive Scarborough Civic Centre, home of the city's municipal government, board of education, and board of health since it was opened by Queen Elizabeth on June 29, 1973.

Its architect was none other than the world-acclaimed Raymond Moriyama, whose designs of such other Metro Toronto showcases as the Central Library at Yonge and Bloor, and the Ontario Science Centre on the western edge of Scarborough, have won dozens of awards.

The architect did not see the Civic Centre as a mere structure, but as a statement about city government. "I was intrigued with the whole notion of how one can extend the questions of democracy at the municipal level," he said. "What is the human relationship between the public and the administration? Between the administration and staff?"

Important questions, but ones seldom asked by the builders of our

The Scarborough city flag is reflected in a mirrored office tower. Photo by Glen Jones

Above: Shoppers flock to the Scarborough Town Centre shopping mall. Photo by Gary Archibald/First Light

Right: Come winter, hardy ice skaters flock to the Civic Centre rink. Photo by Glen Jones

Below: These people take a midday break at Albert Campbell Square. Photo by Glen Jones

Scarborough's growth can be clearly seen from the air. Courtesy, City of Scarborough

major edifices, especially governmental ones. Just as a body without a soul is nothing but flesh and bones, a building without a sense of purpose and an awareness of its role is little more than glass and concrete.

Moriyama created a beautiful building which made the relationship between the city of Scarborough and its citizens perfectly clear. There are no walls, doors, or corridors separating the elected officials from those who elected them. As one critic phrased it, "In the same way that a courtroom shows the power of a judge, the Scarborough Civic Centre emphasizes the power of a people."

People power. Is that not what all members of a democracy want from their political leaders? Accountability, responsiveness to our wants and needs, and the determination to give a damn.

And that is all reflected magically, in the sweeping, swirling interior of the Civic Centre, with its warm, welcoming quality. Over 1,000 men and women work within its stately walls, on five floors that open to a generous atrium.

Just as refreshing is the indoor carp pond and the waterfall flowing outside, a large wading pool, and the fascinating, uneven shale paving of the Albert Campbell Square, named for the man who envisioned a dynamic centre of the city during his many years as its reeve and mayor. He was one of Scarborough's finest dreamers, and well deserves the commemoration.

Art exhibitions go up at the Civic Centre every month, displaying the finest works of local artists and artisans. Concerts are performed every Sunday afternoon, attracting many hundreds of delighted residents. Movies are screened every Tuesday night throughout the summer. Skaters circle all winter on the outdoor rink. Guides conduct tours of the Civic Centre seven days a week. A video called *Scarborough Sphere* is available to tell the story of the city's industries and attractions, as well as how its government works.

The Scarborough Civic Centre was planned as the heart of the city, and the hub of the rapidly developing City Centre steadily growing up around it. The City Centre includes the Scarborough Town Centre, consisting of over 200 stores and services, open over 70 hours every week

Over 1,000 men and women work within the Civic Centre. Photo by Glen Jones

of the year. Other projects have shot up in the area surrounding the Civic Centre in just the past few years, including 100 and 200 Consilium Place, which house the head office for Prudential Insurance in Canada, as well as many other offices. Bell Canada, one of the first major corporations to establish a regional office in the City Centre, owns a six-storey building designed to blend with and enhance the other structures in the area. Canada Centre joins them, a three-phase development project, where the Canadian government provides services for all of Central Ontario. The Canada Life Centre provides office and retail space nearby.

Soon to come to the City Centre is the brand new YMCA. And there are many more projects going up at this very moment, which could well be standing tall while one leafs through this book in the early 1990s:

*At least 1,400 luxury condominiums to be built by Tridel, in at least four buildings in the area of the City Centre.

*Another 1,000 luxury condominiums to be built by Tridel, in association with Prudential Insurance.

*A 400-room Conrad Hilton International four-star hotel, built by

The plaza surrounding Canada Centre offers cool waterfront vistas. Courtesy, City of Scarborough

Prudential and Royal Trust as part of the Consilium project.

*A new, 375,000-square-foot office tower, next to the Hilton.

*Another 375,000 square feet of office space, soon to follow.

*Considerable residential and office space, near the McCowan RT station.

*An office tower to be put up by Royal Bank, also east of the McCowan station.

*A Toronto Dominion Computer Centre, not far from the Canadian headquarters of Toyota, with over 250,000 square feet of space. Toronto Dominion has now joined Scotiabank and the Bank of Montreal in choosing Scarborough to house their nationwide computer centres.

*Just west of Brimley Road and the Scarborough Town Centre, Transmetro is putting up over two million square feet of office, industrial, and commercial development, the first being a 300,000-square foot office building.

*State Farm Insurance, which already owns an important building just northwest of the Town Centre, has more big plans for the area.

*A 220,000-square-foot trade centre and hotel-office-residential complex, part of a major development by a major bank of the People's Republic of China—perhaps its only investment in Canada.

*To the northwest of the City Centre, two office towers will soon go up just across from the Wharton Renaissance Hotel at Kennedy

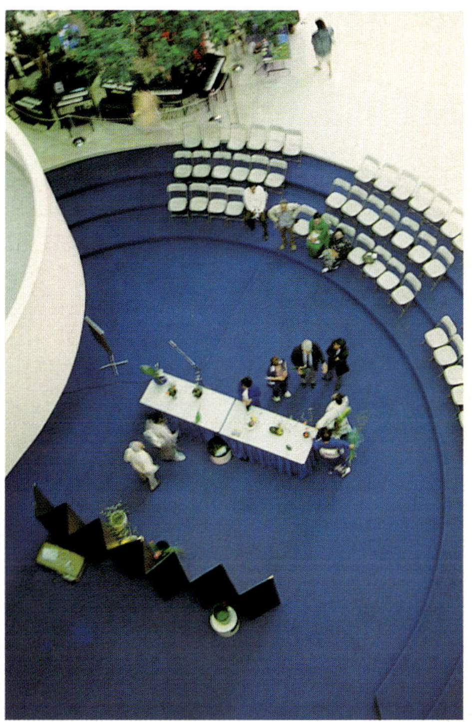

Above: The Japan Week exhibit was one of many events at the Scarborough Civic Centre. Photo by Glen Jones

Left: The Renaissance Hotel makes a stout appearance in downtown. Photo by Glen Jones

Road, each 14 storeys high, with over 400,000 square feet of space in all.

*The national headquarters of Mazda, going up on 10 acres of land to the east of the City Centre. The executives at Mazda are joining Honda and Toyota in Scarborough, along with so many other Japanese companies, from Yamaha Music to JVC.

*Novapharm, one of Canada's major pharmaceutical companies, is also planning more than 200,000 square feet of industrial buildings to the east.

The open fields of the township of Scarborough continue to give way to sleek, tasteful business towers, with all the accompanying prosperity for workers and citizens. Between 1971 and 1981, while the thriving province of Ontario was growing an average of 1.8 percent annually in construction, Scarborough grew 3.3 percent. In finance and insurance, while Ontario grew 6.6 percent each year, Scarborough grew 8.2 percent. Services in the province grew 5.8 percent; Scarborough, 7.2 percent. Public administration jobs increased by 2.4 percent annually in Ontario, while Scarborough more than doubled that rate, at 6.1 percent. In total, while the booming province of Ontario grew an average of 3.7 percent in various fields, Scarborough grew 6.3 percent each year.

All those new jobs mean an expanding population as well, not to mention an ever-increasing tax base for civic improvements. The number of subdivisions registered in Metropolitan Toronto during the first two-thirds of the 1980s, compared with those registered in Scarborough, is equally illustrative:

In 1981, in all other municipalities within Metro Toronto, 18 plans of subdivisions were registered. In Scarborough, there were 30. Continuing this pattern into 1987, there were over a dozen new subdivisions planned in Scarborough, compared with less than one-fourth that many in all the other municipalities of Metropolitan Toronto.

More buildings, more subdivisions, more residents, more jobs. The total number of full-time jobs in the city increased 5.9 percent between 1985 and 1986. And for the third consecutive year, Scarborough was the top performer compared with other municipalities in the area. The growth during this same period in Toronto was a mere 2 percent; in East York, 2.2 percent, and some cities in the metropolitan area actually lost jobs. In the service sector, Scarborough grew 13 percent over 1985-1986, while other cities grew 9.9 percent, 3.6 percent, 2.6 percent, and even lost as much as 15.1 percent.

By 1991 the city of Scarborough estimates that nearly 60 million square feet of industrial space will have been built in the city, adding to the currently available 6.5 million square feet of office space.

Scarborough's goal is that nine out of ten of the people in the labour pool who live in the city should also work in it. With close to half a million residents in 1988, and expectations of over 530,000 by 1995, that means a lot of jobs—and a lot of happy citizens of Scarborough jogging or taking the RT to the office.

It's a great story, and like all great stories, it doesn't end, but keeps on growing, changing, developing. From the Civic Centre to the City Centre to every corner of this exciting young city, Scarborough keeps radiating opportunities, possibilities, jobs, and people.

Prudential Insurance added this airy and whimsical corporate headquarters to the Scarborough skyline. Photo by Glen Jones

Above: Architect Raymond Moriyama designed Scarborough's massive Civic Centre. Photo by Jack Holman

Left: The sun sets outside this arched and airy walkway. Photo by Lorraine C. Parow/First Light

SCARBOROUGH'S ENTERPRISES

CHAPTER TWELVE

NETWORKS

Scarborough's energy, communication, and transportation providers keep products, information, and power circulating inside and outside the area.

Pearson International Airport links Scarborough with the world's major cities. Photo by Glen Jones

THE CITY OF SCARBOROUGH

The award-winning Civic Centre proudly called "the Jewel of City Halls."

Scarborough calls itself "The City of the Future," but in very important ways, even such a futuristic declaration is rather limiting. Because in the City of Scarborough, over the past decade at least, the future has been now. And as the 1980s move rapidly into the 1990s, Scarborough's future has been more "now" than ever.

All this might be pleasantly surprising for the Asians, Europeans, Americans, and any of the many other hundreds of peoples and businesses who have been building and investing in Scarborough over the past several years.

But for the residents of Metropolitan Toronto—of which the City of Scarborough is the fastest-growing and most promising part—this continues to be good news. For decades Scarborough has responsibly progressed. Sure, it had those beautiful bluffs and lots of parks, but it seemed to most residents of Canada's largest metropolis as little more than a burgeoning future city.

Yes, something has clearly happened to the once-borough, now City of Scarborough, which is why a book like this is warranted, and why the news has been spreading so quickly and with such excitement: Scarborough, Ontario, has become, seemingly overnight, the place in Canada, even North America, to build an office or factory, settle one's family, and make a life and future.

But why? Why should a community of fewer than 4,000 people at the turn of the century have more than a half-million today, and be moving so rapidly toward becoming the fourth-largest city in all of Canada?

Let's face it: Every major city has a good fire department; progressive recreation programs and pleasant parks; health services; public and private schools; public libraries; universities and colleges; cultural and entertainment choices; roads, trains, and public transit; and all the other things expected of a good-size metropolis.

Yet the City of Scarborough clearly has something more. It not only has everyday parks, but some of the most spectacular bluffs and nature preserves on the continent, a world-class zoo within its city boundaries, an ethnic mix unrivaled anywhere, and a "downtown" area, located conveniently "uptown" near Highway 401, consisting of more than 120 hectares (300 acres), with thousands of square metres of retail and office space, and, within the next decade, will boast in excess of 40,000 workers—many of them getting to that City Centre via one of the most modern, state-of-the-art rapid transit systems in the world.

Indeed, the sponsors of this book, and its author, have chosen to dedicate entire chapters to many of the above attractions of the City of Scarborough: its educational facilities, hospitals, transportation, communications, ethnic communities, arts and entertainment, its fabulous zoo, even some of its most famous citizens.

But this introduction belongs to the Chamber of Commerce of Scarborough, whose members are understandably pleased to inform as many people as possible as to what has made this city so attractive to business, industry, and the public at large.

There is the Scarborough Council, of course, which is the city's governing body, led by the mayor, with each coun-

The City of Scarborough is one of the fastest growing and most promising communities in Canada.

Scarborough has more available land for industrial, commercial, and office space than most other major cities—some 18 industrial districts and more than 800 hectares (2,000 acres) of zoned land for development, to be more exact—and city leaders are proud to report that all that land will be developed wisely and carefully. As the Economic Develop-

Scarborough is proud of its well-kept streets, transportation system, and fire department.

cil member elected for a three-year term. Once again, this is no surprise, since all cities have elected representatives who legislate policy. But far more than most men and women in such positions, the leaders of the City of Scarborough are profoundly committed to economic growth.

Its mayor of many years has stated, "The staff, public, and politicians all work together in Scarborough, making a political climate where people feel safe to invest in community and economic development."

Scarborough, for all its impressive growth and steadily increasing size, prides itself in having a kind of grassroots government. And the Scarborough Civic Centre is probably the only modern one in the world that has a major frontage of tall, century-old trees along one side. The City Fathers had made a vow when the stunning structure was going up, back in the early 1970s, that the giant, stately trees would be preserved. It is just one of the many examples of how the City of Scarborough is the sort of place that will not allow such a special sense of its eternal past to be frivolously lost.

Like all world-class cities, Scarborough has Works, Planning, and Economic Development departments. Each is highly professional—but, even more important, they all work together in a harmony rarely seen in civic govern-

ments. And precisely because these departments have created such a well-coordinated infrastructure, red tape is continually cut, and development can move ahead both steadily and thoughtfully. As it has.

It is not by chance that Scarborough was named in 1986 as one of the top 10 best administered cities in North America. And hardly a year goes by without one department or another winning an award. Indeed, the marketing programs of the Economic Development Department have won several first-class honors, and the Finance Department captured the Best Budget Presentation Award. The administration of the city is extremely co-operative with hundreds of others around the world, and there is a continual exchange of international ideas going on in the Civic Centre.

ment Department has been saying ever since its creation in 1974: "Business goes where it is invited, and stays and expands where it is well treated."

A catchy motto, and obviously one that is true. Why else would many of the major automobile companies of the world choose to make the City of Scarborough the home of their Canadian head offices? Why else would industries from all over the world—from Japan to Germany, Sweden to Hong Kong, Italy to England, and from right across the United States—be so anxious to want part of their futures in Scarborough?

The staff of Scarborough's Economic Development Department likes to point out that Scarborough consistently outperforms the other cities of Metropolitan Toronto in the attraction

Sun sets on the spectacular Scarborough bluffs.

of new industries, business establishments, and jobs—probably because its mandate includes expediting the development and building processes. "It's the cutting of red tape that does it!" they exclaim, proudly.

And they have good cause to be proud. Of course, at least some credit must be given to the strategic location of the City of Scarborough. Listen to the decision makers of one of Canada's largest companies, who chose to move their head office to this fair city: "It was a chance to get more space, in one of Metro Toronto's finest buildings (smack in the middle of Scarborough's City Centre) at considerably less cost than downtown Toronto, and in a finer-quality building. We expect to save up to $1.2 million annually in rent."

But it still takes more than savings in rental bills to attract the major companies of Canada—as well as a massive labor and clerical force, superb transportation, and some 25 million people a year passing by along Highway 401, observing all the sparkling new buildings and the signs of the major companies. And it takes more than one of the top 10 zoos on earth, and some of the finest recreational possibilities within 100 miles of a major Canadian city. It also takes aggressive marketing on the part of the city, which has created a wide

range of award-winning literature on its business opportunities, mailed out, we might add, from the award-winning Scarborough Civic Centre, proudly labelled "the Jewel of City Halls."

As you'll soon note, this book has a chapter on some of the local heroes

of the City of Scarborough from which we deliberately left one out to look at here: Ben Johnson. At only 25 years of age, this Scarborough resident ran into the history books on August 30, 1987, when he was clocked at 9.83 seconds

The Works, Planning, and Economic Development departments have created a well-coordinated infrastructure that has made Scarborough one of the best administered cities in North America.

in the 100-metre dash. In an event where the world record had been advanced by only 2/100ths of a second in the previous 15 years, Johnson shattered by 1/10th of a second the old mark, and in so doing, won the first gold medal for Canada in track and field at a world championship since 1932.

A crowd of 64,500 saw it in Rome's Olympic Stadium, and another half-billion saw it on television. But perhaps Johnson's greatest thrill—in addition to his being later chosen Canada's male athlete of the year for the second consecutive year in a poll by *The Canadian Press*, and the Lou Marsh Trophy as Canada's outstanding athlete—was the creation of a Ben Johnson Drive in a new Scarborough subdivision.

Providing a good educational system, recreational facilities, and parks is of prime concern to the city fathers as children are one of Scarborough's most important resources.

and a municipal administration that is dedicated to attracting industry and expediting building permits, while creating and maintaining a magnificent community.

This book is subtitled *An Economic Celebration*, but, like the City of Scarborough, is a celebration of business, culture, recreation, education, and life itself.

City of the future? Yes. And the city of now as well.

As you can see, Scarborough is the home of the fastest man on earth, and the fastest human in history. And what community in Canada is growing faster than the city in which he lives? (More than $630 million worth of building permits were granted in 1987, the best year in the city's history.) Yes, Ben Johnson is a fitting symbol of the excellence of Scarborough, with its superior location, lots of space, low taxes, ideal transportation and communications, marvelous quality of life, gigantic labor pool,

Scarborough, with its world-class zoo and breathtaking bluffs, is an attractive place to work and play.

THE PUBLIC UTILITIES COMMISSION OF THE CITY OF SCARBOROUGH

"In electricity and water, we're the only game in town!" comments T.J. Curtis, the former general manager of the long-established and long-respected Public Utilities Commission of the City of Scarborough. What is so impressive about Scarborough's Public Utilities Commission is that its services are actually less costly than its sister commissions in any of the other municipalities in Metropolitan Toronto.

To purchase 1,000 kilowatt hours of electricity per month for a residential consumer in North York, Ontario (the city just to the west of Scarborough), costs nearly 5 percent more than the same service in the City of Scarborough ($57.38 versus $54.75, in 1988). True, for most users it is not equal to the cost difference between a Volkswagen and a Cadillac; but then it is the same, basic service, and the savings can add up—attracting countless residents and businesses to the booming City of Scarborough.

Their secret, if you can call it that, is that The Public Utilities Commission of the City of Scarborough is the only municipality in Metropolitan Toronto that combines those two essential and

The Public Utilities Commission of the City of Scarborough is the only one in the area that combines both electricity and water services. Here power lines are being upgraded to handle the increased loads and reliability.

Commission employees lay water mains to meet the demands made by new subdivisions.

closely related services—electricity and water. By handling both utilities together it makes it less costly to do business in both.

As Mr. Curtis explains it, "We have economy of scale. We have one combined bill, one meter reader, one collection, billing, and accounting department. The savings are passed on to the consumer." A consumer, by the way, who is—unlike the Volkswagen or Cadillac purchaser—a shareholder of the utility. The Public Utilities Commission of the City of Scarborough does not make a profit, but sets rates at levels that will cover both operating and capital costs to provide essential services to one of the fastest-growing cities in Canada.

As its mandate declares, "the Scarborough Public Utilities Commission is the servant of the people, and its sole objective is to provide the residents and their stores and factories with the most efficient and economical service in the supply of water and electricity." Which it has done successfully since 1920. And, while Edmonton, Alberta, grew by 50 percent between 1946 and 1956, and Metropolitan Toronto increased its population by some 40 percent during the same period, the then-Township of Scarborough burgeoned by nearly 400 percent in those 10 years. And the water and electricity services had to increase at the same pace to serve its exploding population.

Nearly 480 employees, from meter readers to office staff and engineers, now work for and with the Commission, meeting the basic requirements of businesses and homes across the City of Scarborough. They are highly efficient. Like all the area's utilities commissions, the SPUC purchases its water from Metropolitan Toronto Waterworks and its electricity supply from Ontario Hydro—these two purchases represent 73 percent of water costs and 85 percent of electricity costs. And yet it still keeps its prices at the lowest-possible level.

The services are essential, and the monies involved monumental. With more than 101,000 water customers and 122,000 electricity customers, the intake revenue is substantial. In 1988 it is estimated that water revenues will exceed $40 million, and electricity revenues will be in excess of $221 million. These ranged from the minimum bimonthly residential bill for 1988 of $20.82 for both water and electricity supply to a one-month industrial bill of $391,000.

As Mr. Curtis notes, "Monopolies need not breed indifference. We have very competitive instincts, and a great pride in what we're doing. We want to give the highest level of service for the lowest-possible cost. And we're doing it." And, he adds, "Scarborough can't grow without us!"

Photo by Glen Jones

Phillips Cables Limited,
120-121

Shorewood Packaging Corpo-
ration of Canada Limited, 122-123

SKF Canada Limited,
124-125

General Motors of Canada
Limited, 126-127

Rex Pak Ltd., 128

Nienkämper, 129

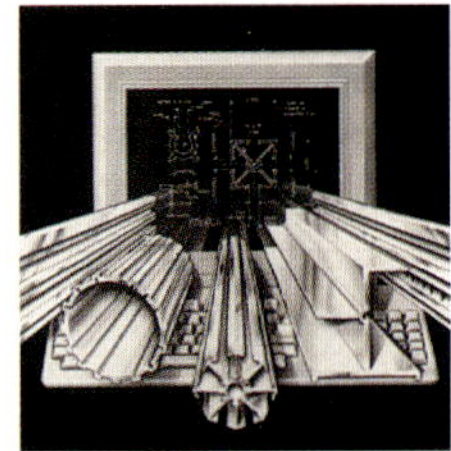

Kaiser Aluminum and
Chemical, 130

Williams Brothers Corpora-
tion, 131

MANUFACTURING

Producing goods for individuals and industry, manufacturing firms provide employment for many Scarborough area residents.

Photo by Gary Archibald/First Light

PHILLIPS CABLES LIMITED

Phillips Cables Limited's latest manufacturing facility opened in 1986 in Moose Jaw, Saskatchewan.

Quality assurance is an integral part of the manufacturing process.

Our modern world increasingly depends on electricity as an energy source for a host of industrial, commercial, and residential requirements. While these applications are varied and diverse, the one element they have in common is that they would not be possible without the wire and cable needed to conduct the electricity.

For nearly a century Phillips Cables Limited has been a leader in the research, design, and manufacture of wire and cable products that provide the essential link between people and technology.

Phillips Cables Limited is a publicly traded corporation, with its head office located in Scarborough's new 100 Consilium building, situated directly across from the Scarborough City Centre. In 1987 the firm's combined domestic and international sales totalled more than $229 million.

Scarborough is also home to one of the company's largest manufacturing facilities, located on Warden Avenue. The plant, established 20 years ago, now employs close to 200 people.

The corporate structure of Phillips Cables Limited encompasses five business units: Power, Construction, and Communication Products; Pyrotenax; and BICC Caribbean. The company currently operates nine manufacturing plants, and each business unit manufactures products for a particular market segment.

Communication Products plants in Vancouver, British Columbia; Rimouski, Quebec; and Dartmouth, Nova Scotia, manufacture communications cable for telephone utilities. Power Products plants in Brockville, Ontario; St. Jerome, Quebec; and Moose Jaw, Saskatchewan, manufacture power cable for a wide range of utility and industrial applications. The Construction Products Divisions' Scarborough plant exclusively manufactures products for the construction industry.

The Pyrotenax plant, located in Trenton, Ontario, manufactures specialized fire-retardant, mineral-insulated electric wiring systems, heating cables, thermoelectric cables, and thermocouples. These highly engineered products satisfy increasing market requirements for safety in operation and continuing performance in

emergency situations.

Phillips Cables' BICC Caribbean plant in Old Harbour, Jamaica, manufactures household wiring, flexible cords, and low-voltage power cable.

This alignment provides maximum responsiveness to market demands for any particular product line, and this market awareness can be traced back to the company's origin.

Phillips Cables Limited was founded in Montreal in 1889 by Eugene Phillips, who was responsible for inventing a machine that would cover bare copper wire with cotton thread—thus fulfilling a market need for insulated wire used for high-voltage electricity distribution.

Since those early days the firm has continued to grow. The company opened its first Toronto sales office in 1903, its Winnipeg sales office in 1910, and its first copper rod rolling mill in Brockville, Ontario, in 1922. During these early decades Phillips Cables supplied some of the first telephone and power cables for use in Canada. Later the company supplied submarine detection and aircraft cable to assist the effort in World War II.

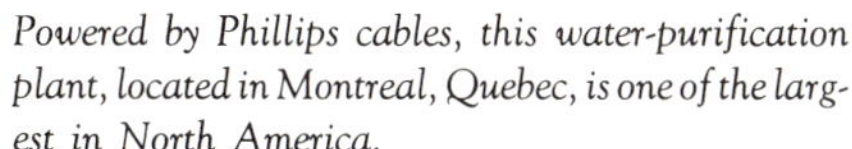

Phillips Cables has also supplied ground communications network cable for the NASA space program.

Today Phillips Cables contracts are as diverse as the world's many needs for electricity, such as being a major supplier to Toronto's SkyDome stadium. Phillips Cables is also the major supplier to Saskatchewan Power's 20-year Rural Underground Distribution Program for electricity. One example of the company's active pursuit of global

Major utilities across Canada use Phillips Cables' underground distribution power cable.

markets is the construction of a cable manufacturing plant under Phillips Cables' project management in Foshan, China.

Over the years, through power cable, construction cable, and communications cable, Phillips Cables Limited has become an internationally respected name among the world's largest electric utilities, manufacturing and resource industries, and communications utilities.

Today wire and cable products manufactured by Phillips Cables Limited can be found in use around the world—in the nations of Europe, the Middle East, the Soviet Union, numerous African and South American nations, China, and countries bordering the Pacific Rim. Phillips Cables is also firmly committed to supplying product to Canada's largest trading partner—the United States.

The 1,500 employees of Phillips Cables Limited are proud to be part of a world-class wire and cable company and of its contributions to life in the modern world.

Powered by Phillips cables, this water-purification plant, located in Montreal, Quebec, is one of the largest in North America.

SHOREWOOD PACKAGING CORPORATION OF CANADA LIMITED

Shorewood Packaging Corporation of Canada Limited is in the vanguard of packaging for the entertainment industry with its record album and cassette covers.

There are many clues to an organization's success, and they often come from the attitude and words of the person at the helm. Some entrepreneurs create something and then become bored and move on. This is most assuredly not the case with Gerry Prochaska, executive vice-president and managing director of Shorewood Packaging Corporation of Canada Limited. His enthusiasm and love for what he has been doing since 1971 is reflected in everything he does—even in a letter he sent to the writer of this corporate profile.

"Enclosed is a short history of our company," he wrote. "The true story of the company, of course, lies deeper in the human element and cannot be explained by dry statistics."

How true. There can be nothing dry about a firm, whether in its statistics or in its products, when it makes a substantial amount of the cassette labels and album covers in Canada; a majority of Kodak film cartons, Jello packages, Vicks cough drops boxes, and much more.

When Prochaska helped to establish Shorewood Packaging of Canada for (and with) Paul Shore of Farmingdale, Long Island, back in the last few weeks of 1970, he began in a leased duplex on Bellamy Road in Scarborough. There were a dozen employees working in a space of 13,000 square feet. Four of those workers are still around, suggesting something about the loyalty Prochaska inspires, and the pleasantness of the operations.

It was an inspired move, as Prochaska, then a plant manager in a division of Sperry Rand, "had to learn everything" so that he would "grow with the company." With nearly $19 million in sales at the end of fiscal 1987, both company and founder have grown significantly. Indeed, Shorewood Packaging of Canada is today in the top percent bracket of packaging printers in Canada.

The venture grew and expanded during the following years. Then, in 1979—the first year Shorewood began to diversify beyond the covers of record albums—Prochaska and his booming business moved to their present location, also in Scarborough, on Midland Avenue, which boasts of more than 107,000 square feet, 150-plus employees, as well as a sales office in Montreal.

From the very start the firm was innovative. For instance, its origins lay in

A variety of the retail products packaging manufactured at Shorewood.

high gloss, diecuts, and strips), and notes that there are only seven machines of this kind on the planet Earth—and all are in Shorewood plants: five in Georgia, one in England, and, of course, this one in Scarborough, Ontario.

No less important to Shorewood Canada is "we care about our employees." Prochaska is pushing for "a form of profit-sharing" as well.

Shorewood Packaging Corporation of Canada Limited has contributed to Scarborough Centenary Hospital, does free promotional printing for the Variety Club, and much more in the community. What seems most satisfying to Gerry Prochaska is that it is "all Canadian-run. We feel very Canadian and are recognized as such, since we have complete autonomy. We can move into new fields and approach new clients, and it's all our own choice." The impressive diversification into food, film, and other kinds of packaging gives credibility to this statement.

a joint venture between Shorewood and CBS Records to "take advantage of new technologies in the manufacturing of record jackets," that had developed during the late 1960s. The company soon moved into "reliable five-day delivery cycles"; three-shift production; priority-order systems that enabled 24-hour deliveries; a comprehensive computerized production control, inventory control, invoicing, and an on-line customer information system (as early as 1974); and an ever-increasing amount of new equipment, as well as research and development.

"What I find so exciting about printing and packaging," the managing director declares, "is that we're involved in what everybody consumes— film, music, food."

Not that Prochaska has done it alone. It is the handpicked cadre of craftsmen and the young, enthusiastic management team that he credits with the lion's share of the success.

In a tour through the mammoth factory of Shorewood its founder points out the gigantic "Josh III" (which prints offset and gravure graphics, then coats

A technician adjusts the high-tech printing machinery.

Packages come in all sizes; here, Jello boxes are diecut.

SKF CANADA LIMITED

SKF's head office and central warehouse building as seen from the 401 Highway.

Ron Starr, the vice-president of SKF Canada's After Market Division, puts it well: "From the man on the street, you'd hear 'SKF who?' Because people don't see or even know about steel or precision bearings. Yet their washing machines and cars depend on them, and so do they! Everything that turns needs a bearing! But because bearings are components and not complete in themselves as consumer products, few appreciate them."

Then let this corporate profile help all those people know: We would be nowhere—and certainly get nowhere—without bearings. SKF of Sweden has 48 bearing manufacturing plants in 13 countries around the world and makes twice as many ball and roller bearings as its closest competitor (and claims one-fifth share of the world market); therefore, one can fairly say that hardly anyone would be getting anywhere without the firm's rarely seen but essential products.

There are only a handful of companies that truly merit the word "international" as SKF does. With sales of nearly 20 billion Swedish Kroner in 1985 (more than $3.5 billion Canadian) the corporation is truly a force to contend with, as its many competitors know all too well.

The origins of this remarkable, international company go back to the turn of the century, when a young Swede developed an innovative bearing for use in the textile mill where he worked. By 1907 he founded his own enterprise, which quickly moved from 15 employees to branches across Europe, all helping—in the passionate words of their corporate history—"in the war against friction around the world."

By 1917 SKF Canada was established—with fortuitous timing. With the war and the burgeoning market in motorcars and consumer products, the demand for antifriction bearings was growing exponentially. The venture began in a small storefront location in downtown Toronto, and soon spread across the country.

Today SKF employs more than 44,000 men and women in offices, plants, and research facilities in some 130 countries worldwide. The major factories are in Sweden, Germany, France, the United Kingdom, Italy, and the United States, but SKF Canada has its own important network: Approximately 140 of its 180 Canadian employees are at the main office in Scarborough, with sales offices in Halifax, Montreal, Scarborough, Edmonton, Winnipeg, and Vancouver.

Canada is, as a great critic once noted, "geographically absurd," and SKF Canada has confronted that problem and conquered it with great success, serving its customers with a remarkably efficient service supply system. (As it must—that boy in the Yukon must have his skateboard; that girl in St. John's her roller skates; those adults in Montreal, Toronto, Saskatoon, Calgary, and Victoria must have their automobiles.) When one thinks of the massive pulp and paper machinery that keep the country—and its

A look inside SKF's automated warehouse.

Scarborough's Rapid Transit train runs on SKF bearings.

economy—running, and the gigantic equipment needed for its mines, one becomes all the more aware of how much bearings of every size, shape, and form are needed.

The distribution warehouse of SKF Canada, which has stared majestically down upon Highway 401 since 1983, has 110,000 square feet of space to accommodate bearings that are transported by the millions in container trucks from European and American factories.

Starr speaks of his warehouse with the pride and affection of a father for a child: "It's one of the most modern, computer-operated packing and sorting centres in the industry," he exclaims. "It's all electronically guided. The computer knows where every product is."

SKF Canada is one of the top two in total bearing sales in Canada, and in the after market—as the vice-president of the After Market Division happily relates—it is by far the largest.

The major Canadian warehousing and distributing company has been firmly ensconced in Scarborough since 1950, when it was attracted by the highly creative Golden Mile of Industry developments. Starr notes, "What has kept us here in Scarborough has been the people. We have a very fine bunch of good and faithful employees." SKF has obviously been good and faithful to them as well, as can be seen by "the many 20-, 30-, and 40-year people who work for SKF Canada."

The organization's brochures relate how the bearings in the single radial engine that powered Charles Lindbergh's *Spirit of St. Louis* were made by SKF—as are the aero-engine bearings of many jets today. However, Canada has its own technological chauvinism: The stunning new Scarborough Rapid Transit (RT), which hooks the thriving city to the rest of the Metropolitan Toronto subway system, rolls along smoothly and trustworthily on bearings made by SKF.

Since before the end of World War I SKF Canada has provided millions of bearings to everything that moves in this country. Today, more than seven full decades later, it is a company that is still very much on the move.

A few of the many types of bearings produced by SKF.

125

GENERAL MOTORS OF CANADA LIMITED

General Motors proudly displays its full-size van.

A history of General Motors of Canada Limited is almost a history of manufacturing in this country, extending back for more than a century. For it was in 1876 that a man named Robert McLaughlin decided that his carriage works in the small town of Enniskillen, Ontario, had to move to a more favorable location if it was to continue to grow. After all, there was no railway nearby, and there was not even a bank in his village. So he decided to move to the bustling town of Oshawa.

And to this day the now-city of Oshawa, just east of the booming now-city of Scarborough, is synonymous with the huge company known as General Motors of Canada. What is less known is that Scarborough also has had a major General Motors auto plant since 1974, producing all the cutaway and diesel vans for the corporation, shipping them to all provinces, with four-fifths of the production going to the United States.

The highlights of General Motors in Canada are interesting to discover since they echo so much of the history of automotive experiences in general, as well as those of our parents and even grandparents. Here are but a few of the key moments:

1907—McLaughlin Carriage Co. signs a 15-year contract for the use of Buick automobile engines.

1915—McLaughlin forms Chevrolet Motor Car Co. of Canada to produce the new Chevrolet 490.

1918—McLaughlin Motor Car and Chevrolet Car companies merge to form General Motors of Canada Limited.

1920—Oldsmobile added to Canadian production.

1926—Pontiac introduced to the line.

1931—Buick introduces its first eight-cylinder engine.

1939—Experimental work on military vehicles is begun, with the first Army trucks produced in 1940.

1943—Production of Canada's 500,000th fighting vehicle celebrated in Oshawa. First Mosquito airplane fuselage reaches production of one a day.

1949—General Motors Diesel of London, Ontario, starts producing diesel-electric locomotives.

1952—Frigidaire Products of Canada plant in Scarborough opens to produce appliances.

1956—Three-millionth vehicle since 1907 is produced.

1961—Four-millionth vehicle produced. Chevy II and Acadian introduced.

1972—Ste. Therese, Quebec, plant converted to Vega production. Eight-millionth vehicle produced in Canada.

1974—The first General Motors of Canada vehicle built in the Toronto area comes off the assembly line at the opening of GM's new plant facilities to produce Chevrolet and GMC vans in Scarborough on the borough's Golden Mile.

1986—The one-millionth van is produced by the Scarborough Van Plant.

And the automobile business goes on. The conversion of the Scarborough plant from Frigidaire products to vans took 10 months to complete, with 16,000 tons of concrete and 2,000 tons of steel used to do it. The plant began at nearly 700,000 square feet in size. From its start in 1974, 15 vans were produced each hour, with more than 400 vans on the assembly line at any one time.

By 1977 there was a major expansion of production facilities in the Van Plant in Scarborough, bringing the total floor space to nearly one million square feet and increasing production to some 25 per hour. Cutaway van production moved up to Scarborough from the United States in 1981, and there were further plant expansions in 1982 and 1983 to accommodate diesel engine options and swing-out cargo doors. In 1986 the plant was expanded once more, this time to allow for throttle-body injected (TBI) fuel systems on all gas engines.

Today some 2,400 hourly workers and another 200 salaried employees work on the 69.5 acres General Motors occupies in Scarborough, on two very busy shifts. Each van travels approximately five kilometres by conveyor as it is put together by the skilled employees of General Motors in Scarborough.

But whether Regular, Sportvan, or Cutaway vans built in the City of Scarborough, or the many superbly designed Chevrolets, Oldsmobiles, Pontiacs, Buicks, Cadillacs, and many more GM products built in Ste. Therese, Quebec, London, Windsor, St. Catharines, and, of course, Oshawa, General Motors of Canada continues to be a major economic and social force in this country.

And its faith shown in its Scarborough Van Plant only emphasizes its commitment to the growing city. From the 154 Buicks built in 1908 to the 347 Chevrolets built in 1915; from the 671 Oldsmobiles built in 1920 to the 224 Cadillacs built in 1923; from the 1,197 Pontiacs built in 1926 to the 3,651 Acadians built in 1961; from the first van built in Scarborough in 1974 to the one-millionth built there in January 1986; and on to the millions more to come—General Motors of Canada Limited marches, and drives, on and on.

A production operator installs an engine in the chassis area.

REX PAK LTD.

Rex Pak Ltd.'s staff, along with Louis Sabatini, have contributed to the growth of the firm.

"It's not just me. It's all the wonderful people here together," says the warm, friendly man in the blue work jacket and white sanitary cap. "Louis can only do so much!"

Still, Louis Sabatini has done plenty since he came over from Italy at the age of 16 with his mother and went to work to support his family. The entrepreneur is now edging into his mid-forties, with two attractive teenagers and a lovely wife. The impressive success of Rex Pak Ltd. underlines the greatness of this country and the City of Scarborough, as well as the industriousness and tenacity of men such as Sabatini. To go from four workers (along with Sabatini and co-founder Doug Napier) in 1974, to 85 employees currently only proves the point. Rex Pak has intricate, electronic, and often self-designed machinery in its 48,000-square-foot factory on Kennedy, south of Ellesmere.

Louis Sabatini lacked "the luxury to go to school," but he had taken trade/mechanical studies back in the "Old Country," so he worked in various industries, setting up machinery. Then—the Canadian Dream at work—he believed that "I couldn't advance any further, and I still wanted to learn. I was getting old (he was 30!) and wondered where I was going."

Sabatini had met Doug Napier in the early 1970s, and the latter, who had sold his packaging company, told him, "I know you're good with machines, and one problem I always had was that nobody knew them. . . ." Napier, being a sales-oriented individual, together with Sabatini formed a perfect marriage, and the two men set up Rex Pak in 1974 with a simple purpose: to package food only, and to give service to new products.

Napier, the first president, passed away in 1982, leaving Sabatini the sole owner and, with the assistance of valued employees, Stephen Napier and John Medeiros, the firm has never had a losing year, packaging coffee creamers, fruit-flavored crystals, hot chocolate, Nutra Sweet products—more than 36 different companies serviced in all. The businesses seem as delighted with Rex Pak as Sabatini is, with his excellent workers and his non-stop growth.

Sabatini buys his machines, but often adds "extras." It is not by chance that "for the type of service we offer, we're one of the largest businesses in the Toronto area. And with our quality control, we feel we're the best in the industry!"

It is amazing to watch the tiny packages zoom along mechanized and even computerized conveyor belts, being filled with the various products.

"We're always looking toward growth," says the president of Rex Pak Ltd. "And the growing city of Scarborough is the place to be."

The dream of becoming a successful entrepreneur has come true for Louis Sabatini.

Louis Sabatini (left) and Doug Napier, co-founders. Napier, the first president, passed away in 1982 leaving Sabatini as sole owner and president.

NIENKÄMPER

When Klaus Nienkämper sold the classic leather and wood sofas and chairs in his New York showroom to the Japanese Embassy in Washington, D.C., the architect was disappointed to hear that he would be "shipping it down from Toronto." He had naturally assumed that the stunning furniture would be European.

Which is one of the main reasons why Nienkämper has been so successful: Always aiming for quality and value has led to such clients as Pierre Trudeau, the National Bank of Westminster, Canadian Pacific, American Express, Labatts, General Electric, and many more of this country's leading individuals and corporations.

Klaus Nienkämper was born in the Rhineland area of Germany, coming to Canada at the age of 20 with the plan to "live here and establish a business." He had studied merchandising, textiles, and furniture in the Old Country, and when he saw "the excellent labor pool" in the City of Scarborough, he knew that this was where he would create his dream.

For the first few years Nienkämper subcontracted others to manufacture his furniture, but since the mid-1970s he has had his own manufacturing facilities, building European-designed furniture under licence, and gradually bringing in Canadian designers as well. Today a full 80 percent of his collection is de-

The Nienkämper Management Plus Series desk and credenza, with mahogany top and details and "granite" finish cases and pedestal fronts, features European style by Canadian designers and craftsmen. The set is shown with an Ambassador chair.

signed by Canadians.

With little advertising the word of Nienkämper's excellence in furniture design spread rapidly. From one employee and sales of "zero" in 1968, there are today more than 100 employees, 60 percent of them craftspeople, and sales of more than $10 million, with a factory of more than 75,000 square feet.

The past few years have seen Nienkämper showrooms opened in Manhat-

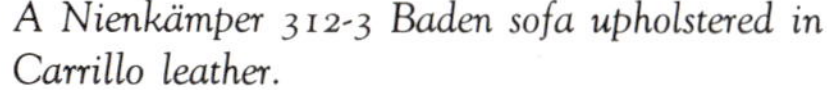

A Nienkämper 312-3 Baden sofa upholstered in Carrillo leather.

tan, Los Angeles, and Chicago, letting the North American business world know that there is superior furniture being made, just above the 49th parallel.

"We are very quality-oriented," says Nienkämper, "creating furniture that provides a quiet background. Business people like the look of stability and permanence, nothing flashy."

Nienkämper creations are not inexpensive, but, as their namesake comments, "I've never been embarrassed to sell something that is costly. We just must make sure that the value is there."

The leather comes from Europe, but all else is Canadian. And with his newest concept, Nienkämper Destinations, for which he and his wife have assembled "a collection of travel bags and adventure furniture with a lifetime guarantee," he has entered the retail market as well.

From his factory in Scarborough—and with a recent offer to open showrooms in Zurich and Madrid—Klaus Nienkämper has proven that magnificent furniture can attract admirers and purchasers from all over the world.

KAISER ALUMINUM AND CHEMICAL OF CANADA LIMITED

Almost anywhere you look there could be an aluminum extrusion component part involved in people's daily living—the lighting fixtures overhead in offices, at the service stations, or in your bank and the buildings themselves. The cars, buses, and trucks, and the bridges they roll over. The windows you look through, pools you swim in, and doors you walk through all use aluminum extrusions for their lightweight, corrosion-free benefits.

Kaiser Aluminum and Chemical of Canada Limited is one of the leaders in the Canadian extrusion industry, and its business has continued to grow year after year because, as sales and marketing manager Terry Porter says, "Aluminum is still the youngest of basic metals used in industry, and it continues to replace older metals and other materials like steel and iron in all types of applications. An aluminum extrusion can be made in almost any shape, and many times it combines several parts into a single piece, which saves assembly time and increases productivity. We had another strong year in 1987, and 1988 looks even stronger as we fill customer needs for improved part performance and innovative production techniques."

Kaiser stays ahead of competition with continued upgrading or addition of plant equipment and facilities. During 1987 new forming, bending, and in-house paint finishing equipment were added, along with additional computerized systems in production planning, quality control, and customer services. "Our goal is to try and help make people's ideas for a part better with an aluminum extrusion."

As a one-source supplier Kaiser controls production from the round aluminum billets up to nine inches in size completely through the extruded

A typical aluminum extrusion application. The seats, upright supports, and ladder components are all produced and painted at Kaiser's Scarborough facility.

shape and including fabricating such as cut to length, drilling, and even subassembly. The firm provides finished extrusions for the construction, automotive, electrical, architectural, and transportation industries.

The operation has been in Scarborough since the early 1950s, but it began to really expand in the following decade, when Kaiser Aluminum of Oakland, California, became involved. Terry Porter and plant and production manger Angelo Bertoia have developed a top-notch, customer-conscious crew of some 150 employees "of many different nationalities and both sexes," who run a round-the-clock operation, providing customers with reliable service and quality products.

Kaiser of Canada is a wholly owned subsidiary, with complete autonomy; all business planning, investments, employee relations, and acquisition programs are handled within the Canadian management team. The total office and complex plant includes some 150,000 square feet in space, which will be expanded to meet the increased capacity requirements as the firm moves on into the twenty-first century.

Most of the aluminum is smelted and refined in Quebec, and most of the employees are from Scarborough, making this a very Canadian company indeed. And as part of a major billion-dollar operation worldwide, Kaiser Aluminum and Chemical of Canada Limited sees a bright future ahead.

Homes, the work place, automobiles, literally everywhere you look people are surrounded by aluminum extrusions, which are used because of their lightweight, corrosion-free benefits. Kaiser Aluminum and Chemical of Canada Limited is one of the main sources for exceptional extrusions, fabricating, and finishing services.

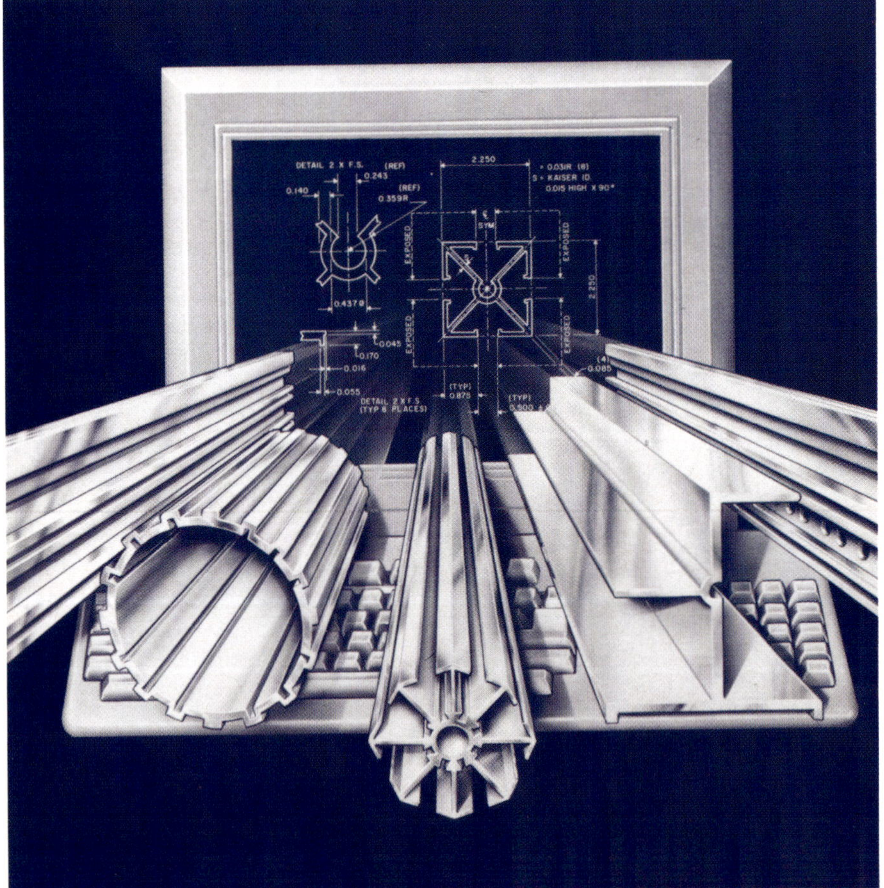

WILLIAMS BROTHERS CORPORATION

George Williams, vice-president and general manager.

There are many family businesses across Canada, but few with such brotherly love and wisdom as the Williams Brothers Corporation of Scarborough. "We've worked together for 30 years, following our father and grandfather into the business," enthuses vice-president and general manager George Williams. "Here's two brothers—one in sales and administration, the other in production. It's a perfect mix."

It is also a perfect example of Canadian ingenuity and business acumen. When Herbert Williams Fire Equipment began in 1908 on Jones Avenue in downtown Toronto, it was basically a service business. The founder, soon joined by his son, went about the growing city recharging fire extinguishers. He even recharged many for free during the tough years of the Great Depression, and years later those firms remembered him with respect and their business.

It was probably the oldest fire equipment company in Canada, but it did not really take off until the second, and especially the third, generations of owners. In 1964 sales were less than $90,000, and there was a staff of seven. Today sales exceed $7 million, with a staff of more than 100 employees—and a recent move to a plant at McNichol and Tapscott doubled the previous 35,000 square feet to 70,000 square feet.

The key to the firm's impressive success was when the family business moved from being service-oriented to a Canadian manufacturer. "My brother, William G. Williams (president), and I saw a market for fire hose cabinets. And every cabinet needs a fire extinguisher."

And so, in 1970 the two brothers "took a giant step and entered the steel fabrication business." The Scarborough firm (the company had moved to the city in 1964) was soon manufacturing safety cans, acid/corrosive storage cabinets, and fire extinguishers for both home and industry. By 1981 it became involved in the export market, "with an invitation from the Ontario government," and today has international sales across the United States—with more than 175 salesmen—and England.

"We're a Canadian-owned company, family run, from humble beginnings," smiles George Williams, "with no subsidies or silent partners, engaging in international sales with giants." Indeed, the organization even bought out a major U.S. company back in 1982 and moved all the stock up to Scarborough. Canadian imperialism in action.

The secret? "It's quality. Ultramodern, pressurized dry chemical and water-type fire extinguishers and other safety products. And we stand behind everything with service." By putting profits back into new dies and equipment—and supporting numerous charities in and around Scarborough—Williams Brothers Corporation has become the largest manufacturer of fire hose cabinets in Canada, and a major force in extinguishers as well.

Hiring minorities and the physically disabled, and working with the Scarborough Board of Education in work co-operative programs has helped the community along with the family corporation.

William G. Williams, president.

Monarch Investments Limited, 134-135

ScotiaMcLeod, 136

The Prudential Insurance Company of America, 137

Clarkson Gordon, 138

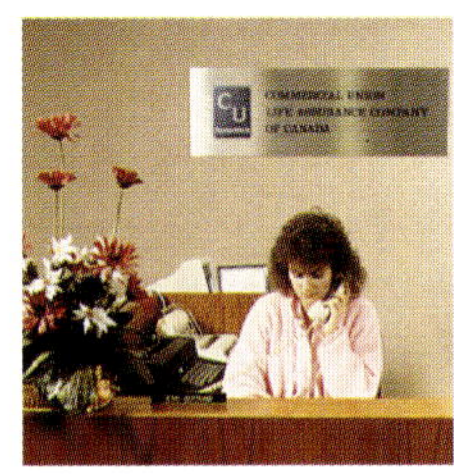

Commercial Union Life Assurance Company of Canada, 139

Command Records Services Limited, 140

CHAPTER FOURTEEN

BUSINESS AND PROFESSIONS

Greater Scarborough's professional community brings a wealth of service, ability, and insight to the area.

Metro East is one of the growing number of corporations building towers in Scarborough. Photo by Glen Jones

MONARCH INVESTMENTS LIMITED

This lovely Henry Summerfeldt-designed home is the most popular model in The Bridle Trail development in Unionville.

When one drives through the City of Scarborough there are entire residential areas that catch the eye. One of the most beautiful is Chartwell, filled with gorgeous homes, wonderfully designed and laid out in a handsome neighborhood. But behind most planned areas is a business story, and the firm behind Chartwell is Monarch Investments Limited, one of the most respected development and building companies in Canada.

Today Monarch is publicly traded and is part of a major British firm, developing properties all over the globe. But like many companies it began small, with no hint of its future as a builder of quality homes. During World War I a group of Toronto lawyers got together and began financing stock enterprises, soon acquiring the assets of a real estate corporation, Monarch Realty.

By 1921 Monarch Mortgage and Investments Limited was formed to deal with second mortgages. But the Great Depression soon made that field rather tenuous, leading in 1939 to the wise decision to build houses under the name Monarch Construction and Realty Limited.

It has been steady and exciting growth since then. Monarch Investments Limited was purchased in 1955 by a major international company out of London, England—Taylor Woodrow—and its top-quality homes stand proudly across Ontario (in such places as Ottawa, London, St. Catharines, Markham, and, of course, Scarborough), into Quebec, and even as far away as Houston, Texas, and Atlanta, Georgia. There are attractive shopping centres across Ontario as well, including Scarborough's Chartwell Shopping Centre, which is being expanded by 40,000 square feet in 1988, reflecting its success.

In the words of vice-president G.A. Deslauriers, "We cut our teeth on better-quality homes in the Agincourt area of Scarborough, acquiring farms on the east side of Midland." The time was the late 1950s, when what was then still a borough was small and sleepy, but very promising to enterprising companies such as Monarch.

The firm slowly and carefully put up in excess of 2,500 quality, single-family homes, calling the development Chartwell, and by the early 1980s it was putting up an additional 1,500 homes in another area christened Upper Chartwell. People who waited to buy will be heartsick to read that these attractive homes were selling for less than $25,000 three decades ago, and today fetch prices in the range of a quarter-million dollars each. And they are worth the latest price, according to local wisdom.

From 1970 on Monarch began to build neighborhood shopping centres on the land it owned adjacent to the homes, recognizing that there was more advantage to building them as part of the company portfolio, rather than selling the valuable land to others. At the time of this writing Monarch is going through the zoning process to build one of its largest shopping centres next to Upper Chartwell, at Steeles and Midland.

"There's no question that we are the prime, ongoing builder of single-family quality homes in Scarborough," claims Deslauriers proudly, adding that the firm has "an ongoing commitment to expand our American operations. Yet we are a cautious, conservative company." Cautious, perhaps, but profits suggest otherwise. In the 15 years that Deslauriers has been with Monarch, he notes happily, profits have expanded from one million dollars to $20 million a year.

Most important is the reputation Monarch has—and one that, truly, money could not buy. "We really do have a fetish about quality," explains Deslauriers, "and for good-value, carefully built homes." Success only proves his point. It was the first company with "visible customer service trucks," and the first to have "a fully organized, well-staffed customer service department." How busy they are—or are not—is revealed by one salient fact: Most of the organization's subcontractors have been with Monarch for better than a decade. And we all know how difficult it is to find a good craftsperson nowadays.

In the early 1980s Monarch Investments Limited purchased an old, family-run company named A.B. Cairns, which also had a solid reputation for building fine homes in the Scarborough area. It is a wholly owned subsidiary, and, says Deslauriers, "We've chosen to carry it on, under the same excellent tradition, and under the same name."

The superior construction continues: Monarch is presently putting up more than 1,200 quality homes in Unionville, Ontario, not far from Scarborough, continuing to spread the good word and the quality homes. "We've always stressed that we build communities," declares Deslauriers, and the thousands of happy home-owners across Ontario, Quebec, and even the southern United States, all appear to agree.

Scarborough was once known as a blue-collar area, but thanks to firms such as Monarch Investments Limited, its spacious boundaries include more than 4,000 exquisite homes—and several attractive shopping centres—that have made the city look more white-collar, and even pinstriped, than most of Metropolitan Toronto.

Centrally located in the community, The Bridle Trail Shopping Centre reflects Monarch's policy of building a whole community with residential and commercial complementary architecture.

SCOTIAMcLEOD

There are some businesses that are one of a kind. More common are those with a number of competitors in the same field, all vying for the same clientele.

One such firm is ScotiaMcLeod—the new name of McLeod Young Weir Limited. The firm is now a part of the Bank of Nova-Scotia's family of companies, and the new name and company logo are in recognition of its association with Scotiabank. For a highly respected investment firm, Canadian-based (with offices in every province) but internationally represented (in such far-flung places as New York City, London, Zurich, and Tokyo), ScotiaMcLeod faced a problem that is more complex than the myriad investments it offers: Why should customers deal with the firm?

After all, although ScotiaMcLeod is one of the top investment dealers in all of Canada, and has zoomed from around 100 salespeople in 1980 to more than 600 investment executives just seven years later, it still offers most of the same products and services as other major firms in the field: It buys and sells stocks and bonds, handles Registered Retirement Savings Plans, and offers investment advice and services to individual, corporate, and government clients.

One answer, naturally, was to move to the fastest-growing city in Canada and plant a flag—or branch, if you prefer—on the fourth floor of the impressive and handsome Consilium Two, just across from the Scarborough Town Centre, in the city's downtown core.

The decision has worked out surprisingly well, as the youthful manager of the branch, Stuart Livingston, is more than eager to share. "We believed that the way this city was growing, we just had to have a presence here," he says, smiling with enthusiasm. "We had to go where the people were."

The people were clearly in Scarborough, Ontario, and they were obviously as happy to welcome the new branch of ScotiaMcLeod back in 1984 as the 2,000-employee-strong firm was anxious to serve them. When the Scarborough office of ScotiaMcLeod opened, there was one manager and one

Stuart Livingston, manager.

salesperson. Today there are 11 salespeople, with manager Livingston "looking to grow beyond that," possibly by another 50 percent before the decade is over.

The Scarborough office is one of the largest in sales in the entire Ontario region. Stuart Livingston radiates confidence and enthusiasm.

ScotiaMcLeod has a "very, very good research department," according to Livingston, "a very creative corporate underwriting department, state-of-the-art technology," and, certainly important, "we're very involved in the Scarborough community."

ScotiaMcLeod was the first brokerage firm to have a branch office in Scarborough. To paraphrase a famous saying, "The early bird has been busy investing."

THE PRUDENTIAL INSURANCE COMPANY OF AMERICA

"Prudential saw Scarborough as the future," says Ron D. Barbaro, president of the company's Canadian operations, which is why it developed the striking Consilium project just across from the Scarborough City Hall. And, since August 1985, the new headquarters for Prudential in Canada has stood proudly in 200 Consilium Place.

Not that such involvement in Canada was anything new for the famed Prudential Insurance Company of America, which is the largest non-bank financial institution in the world. In fact, it has been active in Canada since 1909, and has had its Canadian head office in Toronto since 1950.

The Consilium project was "the largest single real estate deal that Prudential has been involved with in Canada," with the entire development approaching a half-billion dollars. This means that some $5.8 billion is now invested in Canada, nearly three times what had been invested just a dozen years ago.

With its acquisition of Bache Securities, The Prudential has further increased its range of financial services to Canadians. "Our basic approach is to be a full-service, multi-lines company. For many years we concentrated on life and health insurance," says Barbaro.

200 Consilium, the new Canadian head office of The Prudential Insurance Company of America.

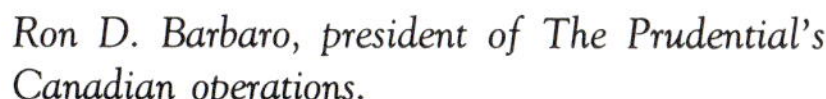

Ron D. Barbaro, president of The Prudential's Canadian operations.

"Today we sell mutual funds, home and auto insurance, and many other products."

A committed Canadian nationalist, Ron Barbaro spent more than 30 years in the insurance business as both a salesman and a broker before becoming Prudential's president in 1986. He was the first Canadian president of the industry's prestigious Million Dollar Round Table, and truly knows the business inside out.

Prudential has always seen fit to put its money where its policyholders are: Back in the early 1970s a *Toronto Star* headline read "Prudential Plows Profits Back Into Our Economy," and how true it was. By the end of 1974 The Prudential had invested more than $2 billion in Canada, of which $1.3 billion came from Canadians insured by the company, and $860 million from U.S. nationals.

Today The Prudential has more than 100 offices across Canada and in excess of 2,500 employees, which includes a field force of some 1,000 insurance representatives. Its operating results are as impressive as its superior service and name.

"Prudential is perfectly poised to meet the challenges created by Canada's rapidly expanding financial services industry," says Barbaro. "We intend to be a dynamic leader of this industry, aggressive in our pursuit of excellence and uncompromising in our commitment to our customers."

137

CLARKSON GORDON

In a recent statement on "Our Mission," the partners at Clarkson Gordon (one of the largest firms of chartered accountants in this country), proclaimed their desire to be "the leading, most respected, and successful public accounting and management consulting firm in Canada." With the leadership shown in its setting up the Scarborough office in the summer of 1977, the company seems well on its way to achieving that goal.

Beginning as Thomas Clarkson and Company in Toronto in 1864, and adding Colonel Gordon's firm in 1913, Clarkson Gordon has grown to an organization of more than 3,000 men and women in 25 offices across Canada. Its services include not only the traditional services of accounting, auditing, and taxation but also, with its associated firm, Woods Gordon, all aspects of management consulting.

An impressive company, but all the more impressive when one looks at its brief but exciting history in the City of Scarborough, Ontario. Back in the mid-1970s Thomas Abel was the assistant managing partner of the Toronto office of the firm, and was involved with establishing new offices for Clarkson Gordon. "I volunteered to open an office in Scarborough for two reasons," he notes today. "To provide better, closer service for our suburban clients, and to be more readily available to potential clients in a rapidly developing area who would not go downtown for their accounting and consulting needs but still want to work with a

Tom Abel and Jim Boyko deal with a matter informally in the reception area.

major firm."

Clarkson Gordon became the first of the Big Eight Canadian chartered accounting firms to locate in Scarborough. An important strategy involved recruiting staff from the local area. As Tom Abel puts it, "We're in a people business, and we must be close to our clients. So we have the resources of a big firm with the personal relationship of a small office." Not so small anymore—the original 20 has more than doubled in the first decade in Scarborough.

The Scarborough office also services clients in Markham, Pickering, Ajax, Whitby, Oshawa, even Belleville

All Clarkson Gordon staff find that portable micros are essential for providing effective service.

and Peterborough. With a special emphasis on meeting the needs of growing owner-managed and entrepreneurial clients, including high-technology companies, the office is expanding right along with them. A substantial portion of the office activities involves helping new and growing businesses develop business plans, obtain financing, and resolve taxation matters.

Being the first such firm in Scarborough has led its partners and staff to "pride ourselves on involvement in the community." Senior partner Tom Abel helped create what is today the Scarborough Chamber of Commerce, as well as Arts Scarborough; partner Jim Boyko was the first president of the Scarborough Estate and Financial Planning Council; and partner Brian Wallace just retired as president of the Markham Board of Trade.

Managing partner, Ron Buckle, who is chairman of the Scarborough Chamber of Commerce Entrepreneurial Development Committee, sums up the local feeling well when he states, "We take our clients' business personally, and this reflects our entrepreneurial spirit and our commitment to help develop the great potential in Scarborough."

COMMERCIAL UNION LIFE ASSURANCE COMPANY OF CANADA

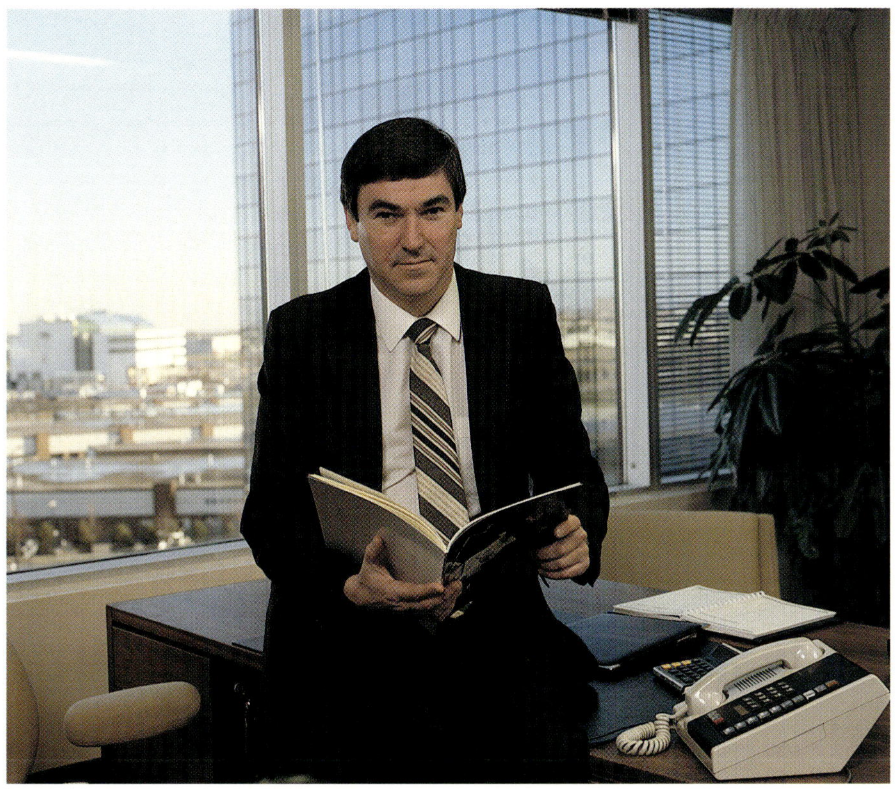

H. Bruce Gordon, president.

There are some companies that are old and others that are quite new. But rarely does one encounter a single firm that is so old and yet so new as Commercial Union Life Assurance Company of Canada.

In the worldwide Commercial Union Group of Companies is Hand in Hand Fire & Life, which began back in 1696. And another marvelous historical fact: One of the Commercial Union companies, back in 1807, declined a policy for one Napoleon Bonaparte, having come to the conclusion that he was "a questionable risk." How right they were.

And how contemporary some of the firm's actions are. For although the mother company back in England chose to found an agency office in Montreal way back in 1863—it did not move into the United States until 1869, concerned over the unrest there from the Civil War—it actually was very recently that a truly Canadian Life company was created: January 1, 1984. It was then that the Commercial Union Life Assurance Company of Canada was formed—a Canadian firm registered under the Canadian and British Insurance Companies Act.

Not that it was insignificant before that. The Canadian operation actually began in 1961 as a branch of the United Kingdom parent and grew, in just 16 years, from less than a quarter-billion dollars in life insurance to well in excess of $4.5 billion.

"We decided to become a domestic company," says vice-president Myles Bunting. "We had to do that to expand. So we're now in a much better position to grow."

In the past Commercial Union Life operated as a composite, writing both life and general insurance. It is in the top 10 in Canada in the latter, and in the top 20 percent in the former. But the life segment became more autonomous, and it was eventually decided that they would no longer operate side by side.

That is why Commercial Union Life moved to Scarborough in April 1985, becoming the first major tenant in the beautiful 100 Consilium building, across from the Town Centre. There are already more than 150 employees on the operation's 1.5 floors, containing 27,500 square feet of space, with 50 more staff from coast to coast.

"We came to Scarborough since we were looking for an expanding business centre," says president Bruce Gordon. "We saw the city as a rapidly developing community that would attract many clients. And we feel that we can attract and retain the staff we need to grow in life insurance by being here in Scarborough."

The business' projections call for $100 million in revenue by the end of 1988, with another $300 million in invested assets. Also, "because we're smaller, we can be more flexible and offer more services than gigantic companies," says Gordon.

"We hope to grow rather aggressively," claim both Bunting and Gordon. Commercial Union Life Assurance Company will continue to build on its rich history.

The reception area of Commercial Union Life.

COMMAND RECORDS SERVICES LIMITED

Command Records Services Limited has secure buildings, such as this one, throughout Metropolitan Toronto as well as London, Ontario, and Halifax, Nova Scotia.

The idea behind Command Records Services Limited is so obvious and simple that its extraordinary success comes as no surprise. After all, information is at the centre of society; records have to be kept, protected, retrieved, and, yes, even destroyed. For two decades Command has done it all, with an efficiency and competency that has made it not only number one in the industry, but even that industry's creator in Canada.

Command began in the fall of 1968 as a records management consultant firm, but it grew as quickly and surely as all those boxes in a business' basement or attic. "Security is big," notes president Gordon Joyce, "as is records retention and disposal. We destroy more than 3,000 tons of documents every year."

In addition, clients have economical and security backup of their critical data, ensuring that a local or regional disaster would not mean the end or a serious disruption of their business. But more than that—"If someone errs in their office, we provide up-to-date duplicates of their vital records, so we're a support system to computers as well."

Growth has been rapid, according to Joyce, and in early 1987 Command joined the Moore Group of Companies with a rather impressive mandate: "To expand our business throughout the Free World." And the firm will do it too, since its services perfectly complement those of Moore, which is the world's largest business forms manufacturer. So today Command covers the entire life-cycle of a document, from its creation, through its storage, retrieval, eventual destruction, and rebirth. Ecology thrives in the business world, as well.

Gordon Joyce is a proud Scarborough resident, as are Ron Webb, vice-president/sales and marketing, and Jack Shier, the recently retired secretary/treasurer. Joseph Hamilton, vice-president/operations, and Rogers Bell, the new secretary/treasurer, round out the senior management team.

Gordon Joyce's burgeoning business has done much to make the city grow. By January 1971 the organization had its first building. As of today there are more than a dozen locations sprinkled across Metropolitan Toronto, as well as London, Ontario, and even Halifax.

These buildings hold one million spaces, belonging to some 1,500 accounts, which includes many of the top 500 companies in Canada. "It's like running a condo complex for one million people," grins Joyce.

And he has good cause to grin. Command Records Services Limited, after a recent acquisition, is now represented coast to coast with more buildings across Canada, so its 100 staff members, by 1988, should be increased to 250. And if the company lined up all the boxes of files, they would run well past 220 miles.

With more than four dozen vehicles; nearly 500,000 square feet of buildings; a rapid 24-hour retrieval system; computer, tape, and paper storage; and more, "It's a solution to management's paper and information problems," says Joyce.

Command has one million spaces storing records for some 1,500 accounts, all accurately indexed for speedy retrieval.

Tridel, 144-147

Beverley Hills Home Improvements, 148-149

Trilea Centres Inc., 150-151

Herity Group of Companies, 152-153

Runnymede Development Corporation Limited, 154

Royal LePage Real Estate Services Ltd., 155

Lebovik Enterprises Limited, 156

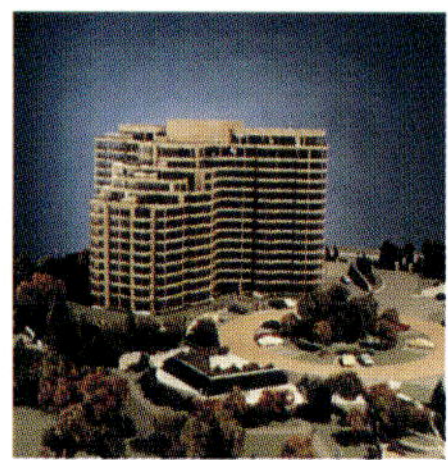

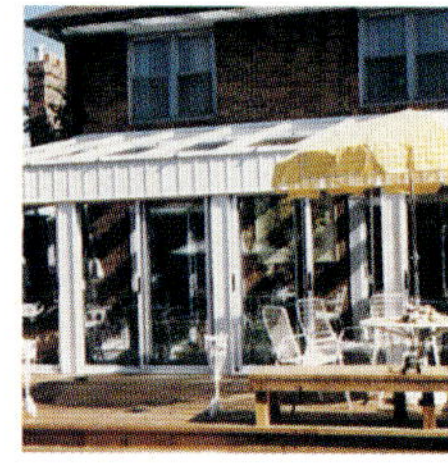

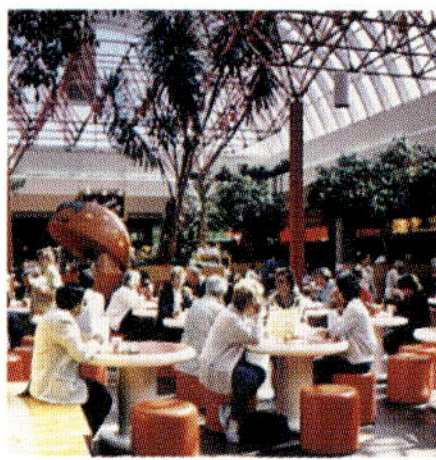

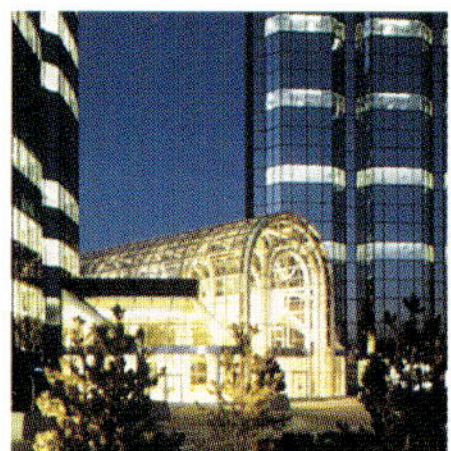

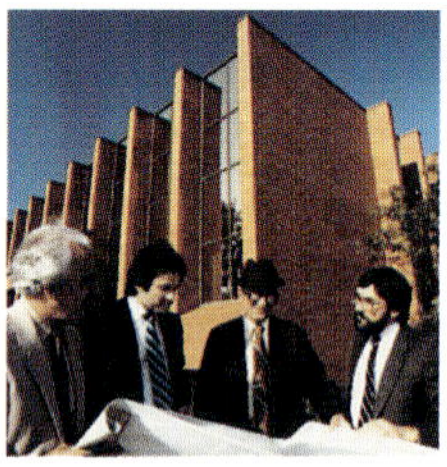

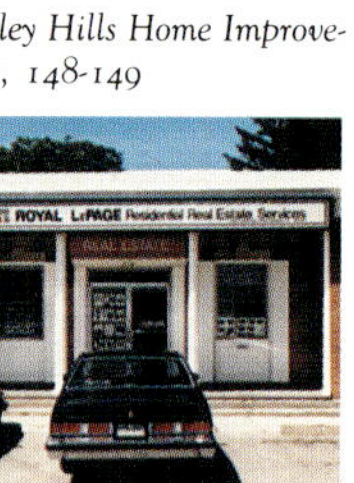

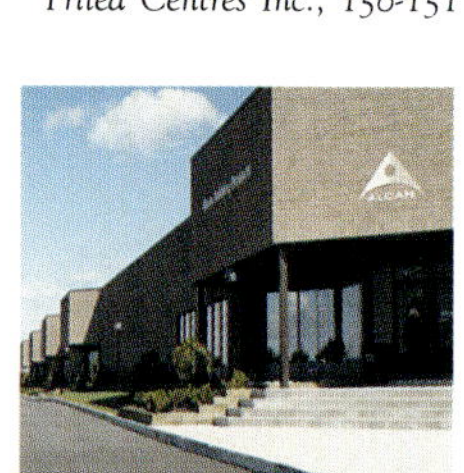

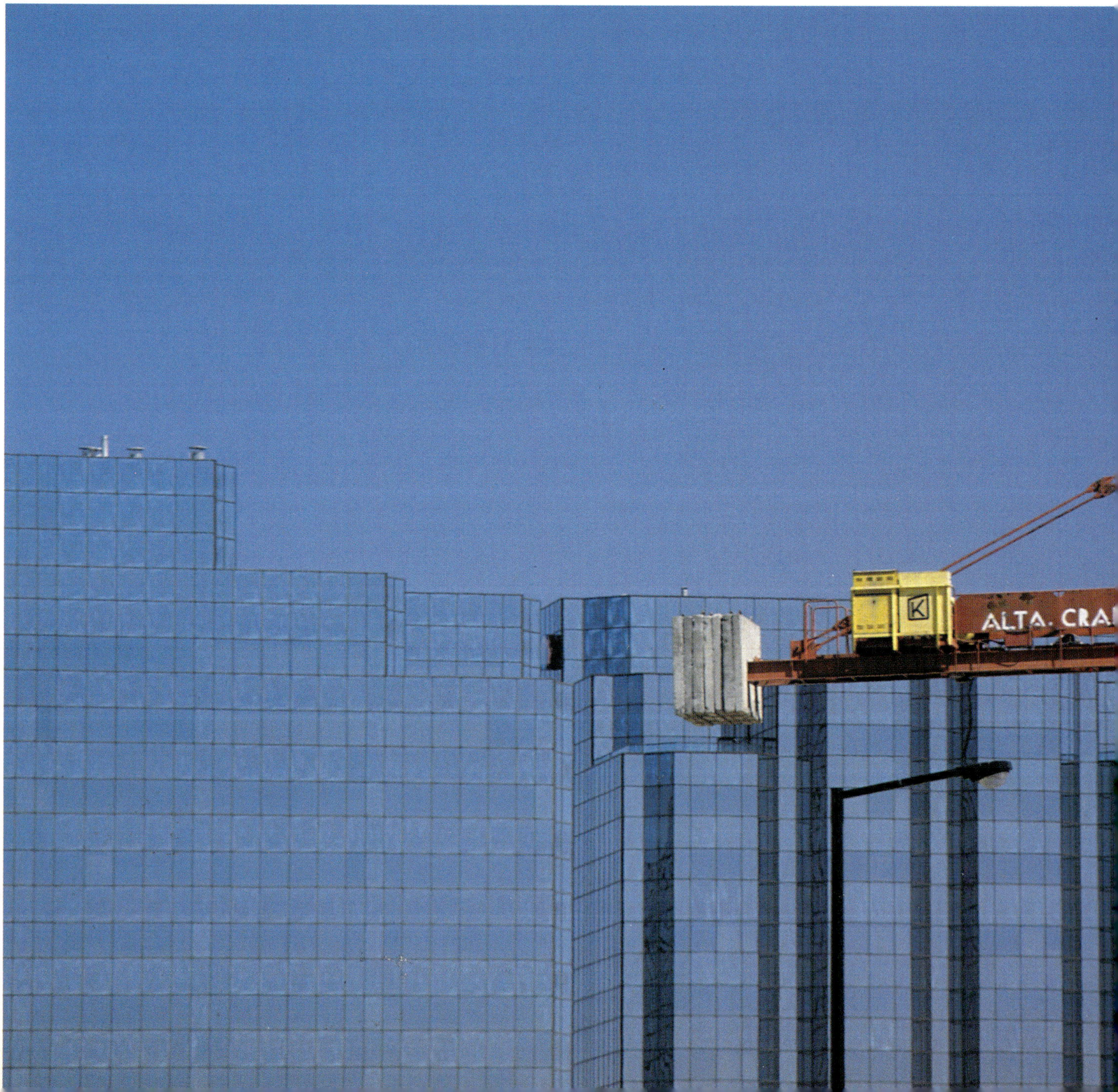

CHAPTER FIFTEEN

BUILDING GREATER SCARBOROUGH

From concept to completion, Scarborough's building industry shapes tomorrow's skyline

Corporate construction continues in Scarborough. Photo by Glen Jones

TRIDEL

Tridel has been having a love affair with Scarborough for more than two decades. In fact, Tridel earned its well-deserved reputation for dependability and excellence in Scarborough with such popular and beautifully designed buildings as Skygarden, Wedgewood Grove, Skypark, Bridletown, and Royal Crest—buildings that now contribute to the growing Scarborough skyline. "We go back together a long way," smiles John McDonald, vice-president/sales of Tridel, "so to contribute to an economic celebration book about Scarborough is a genuinely delightful experience for us."

Tridel is a proudly Canadian company, creating homes of unrivaled quality and workmanship for and with Canadians. The late Jack Del Zotto, a bricklayer by trade, laid the foundations of the company in 1934 when he built his first home in Toronto. He soon had a small, thriving business called Del Zotto homes that concentrated on the construction of single-family homes. Then, in the late 1960s, with the assistance of his three sons, Angelo, Elvio, and Leo, the company moved into new territory—adult-life-style condominium residences—and Tridel was born. The rest, as they say, is history. In 1986 the firm began trading publicly, listed on the Toronto Stock Exchange as Tridel Enterprises.

Today Tridel is the largest and most respected residential condominium developer in Canada with literally thousands of suites across the Metropolitan Toronto landscape. From Pickering to Mississauga, from Unionville to downtown Toronto, Tridel condominiums can be found. But this leader in the condominium industry has never forgotten its roots. Tridel came of age with Scarborough, and the love affair between the two continues.

As more and more people are discovering the diversity and excitement that is Scarborough, the demand for elegant homes grows accordingly. Tridel has responded by providing carefully planned and unique condominium dwellings throughout Toronto's flourishing east end, with six major projects currently in development.

One of the many reasons why this Canadian success story has become the national industry leader in condominium development and construction is because its designs and strategies are constantly adjusted to meet shifting

public tastes and needs. Before Tridel commits itself to a new project, extensive discussions are conducted within the community to determine just what people are looking for. Each development is then designed to conform to the requirements of both the purchasers and the particular neighborhood.

A perfect example of this philosophy is Greystone Walk, located at the corner of Danforth Road and Midland Avenue. This successful project demonstrates the intense preconstruction involvement between Tridel and potential purchasers. Because Tridel's in-depth research determined there was a huge void to be filled, the company planned Greystone Walk to appeal primarily to the first-time buyer. The whole complex has been designed to correspond to what this often overlooked segment of society wanted in a first home. In addition, Greystone Walk will revitalize an older area of Scarborough by providing badly needed convenient retail facilities as well as three striking residential buildings.

From the outset Greystone Walk was a triumph. In fact, this new adult-life-style condominium was so successful that within six weeks the first phase was virtually sold out. This is really not

surprising when you consider that Greystone Walk offers a fabulous life-style at affordable prices. By the summer of 1989 the initial building should be ready for occupancy—an attractive new addition to an older area of Scarborough.

At the other end of the spectrum there are many people who already own large, traditional homes but now, with their children grown, want to participate in a leisurely adult condominium life-style. To accommodate their needs for larger and more luxurious suites, Tridel has conceived the Gates of Guildwood, a majestic, nine-acre complex that will consist of two luxurious buildings joined underground by an extensive recreational centre—The Guildwood Club.

Nestled high on the hill overlooking Guildwood Village, this will cer-

idence of choice for Scarborough citizens. There are marble floors in every foyer and marble vanity tops in all bathrooms. Each suite is designed so that windows seem to envelop the occupant, with magnificent views surrounding the building. Some even have expansive terraces, including those on the impressive two-storey penthouse level.

Guildwood Village itself is one of the best kept secrets in the Metropoli-

tainly be one of the preeminent addresses in Scarborough. It is the stunning terraced design of this project, however, that seems to have captured everyone's imagination. The Gates of Guildwood has been planned to maximize exterior wall space, so even those suites on the lower floors will possess a breathtaking view. Residents with a southern exposure will be able to gaze out over the Scarborough Bluffs and Lake Ontario, while the northern view will be an expanse of greenery, courtesy of the Scarborough Golf Course. For sailors and golfers, the Gates of Guildwood is the next best thing to heaven.

Although the exterior of this project is impressive, the design and layout of the suites themselves have helped make the Gates of Guildwood the res-

tan Toronto area. Just minutes away is the Guild Inn and its grounds—several acres of Canadian history waiting to be discovered.

But it's not only the location, price, and suite designs that make Tridel condominiums so attractive to today's busy adults—it's the wealth of recreational facilities right on their doorstep. Different projects feature different leisure-time amenities depending on what age group is being targeted. Tridel buildings include such luxuries as indoor and outdoor swimming pools, whirlpools, racquetball and squash

these chores.

Even though Tridel is now a multimillion-dollar enterprise, it's important to note that it is also committed to contributing to the city it helped shape. Countless charities and community activities have been supported by Tridel, from Little League hockey teams to such prestigious organizations as the Scarborough Arts Council. Enhancing and strengthening the Canadian way of life is how Tridel touches each family.

For more than two decades Tridel has been having a love affair with Scarborough. During this time Tridel has grown from a small and successful family business into a multimillion-dollar enterprise employing hundreds of people, while Scarborough has grown from a borough of Toronto into a vibrant, multifaceted city that thousands proudly call their home.

Tridel is truly a Canadian story—the personification of the Canadian dream. This is a dynamic, resourceful company dedicated to making dreams come true—today and tomorrow.

courts, saunas, tennis courts, fully equipped exercise rooms, party areas and lounges, hobby area, libraries, sundecks, billiards and video rooms, and beautifully landscaped grounds with barbecue areas and quiet walkways. Many have professional staff to organize social and fitness programs and events. There are even office spaces and boardrooms available for the unrepentant workaholic.

Another appealing facet of condominium living is independence: the freedom to just lock your door and leave for that vacation without worry. Many buildings have concierges and electronic surveillance systems; indeed, some even have manned gatehouses. All provide peace of mind whether you're at home or away. Gone too is time-consuming, aggravating, and often expensive home maintenance. Never again will you throw your back out shovelling snow or mowing lawns—the property management and maintenance teams are on hand to perform

BEVERLEY HILLS HOME IMPROVEMENTS

Stan Greenberg, president.

The name of Beverley Hills Aluminum Sales and Installations Ltd. was misspelled on its application for incorporation, but there have been no mistakes made since. Begun in a Scarborough basement in May 1977, with its president doing all the office work, the venture had sales of $125,000 in its first year. In 1987 sales topped $17 million, and the firm currently employs 150 installers, 25 salespeople, an office staff of 50, and 20 part-time workers. Today Beverley Hills is the number-one renovative dealer in the Toronto area in the home improvement field of additions, siding, windows, and doors—and, according to Alcan Aluminum, the largest home improver using its products on the continent.

Stan Greenberg—the founder of Beverley Hills Home Improvements — is only moving into his mid-thirties now, and the only real clue from his appearance to his inspired entrepreneurial skills is the image suggested by his rolled-up shirt sleeves. To build a business from zero to many millions of dollars in sales in only a decade has taken a lot of rolled-up shirt sleeves and a lot of good, honest hard work.

Greenberg was born in Montreal in late 1953 and studied business administration at that city's Dawson College for two years. He then moved to Toronto, while still in his teens, and worked for various major firms in purchasing—surely a superb background for a future aluminum siding investor, including Meridian Developments, Canada Carbon & Ribbon, and the Metro Toronto Zoo. "I was always aggressive," he says.

Then came the idea to establish his own business, in which he would sell and install siding, eavestroughing, soffit and fascia, storm doors, windows, shutters, and much more. "I wanted a name with class," Greenberg recalls, referring to the prestigious, if misspelled, name of his firm, "since we were virtually unknown."

His passion for excellence and success, as well as his willingness to work 18-hour days for the first several years, were the major factors in the growth of the enterprise. He had "absolutely no expenses" at the start, installing an extension phone into his unfinished basement and purchasing a used desk for $50.

The young businessman began by making "cold calls" (walking house to house). "I even did a job that paid two dollars," he laughs. "I put some weatherstripping on a guy's door." The $100,000 additions to homes, and the tens of thousands of dollars' worth of work for Ontario Housing and Sunnybrook Hospital—along with thousands of other major projects—would come later.

The impressive first-year sales

This addition by Beverley Hills Home Improvements provides year-round comfort.

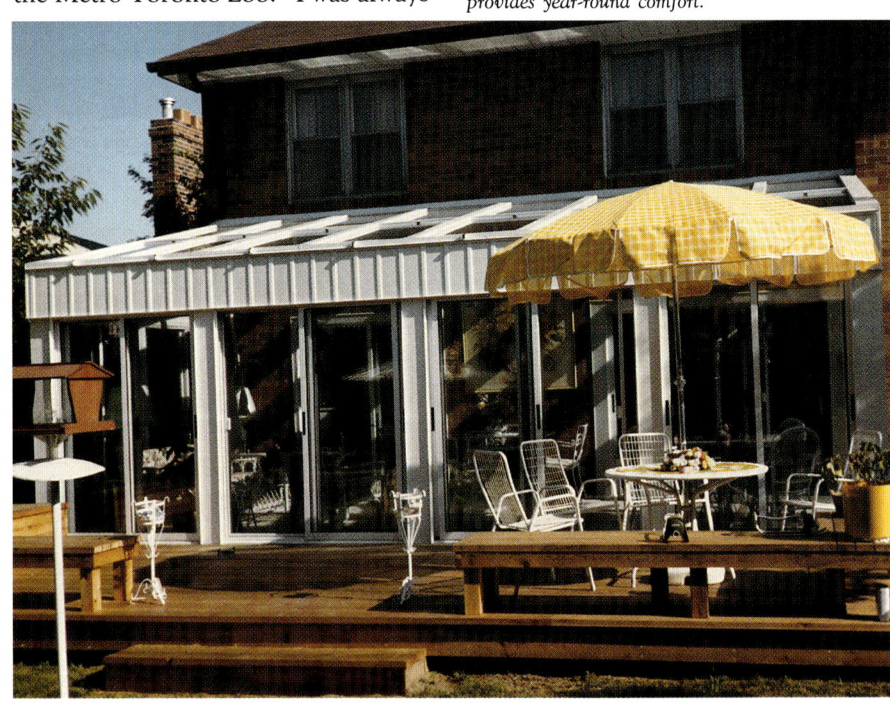

doubled to $250,000 in the second year, then to one million dollars in the third. Beverley Hills was selling/installing more than $3 million worth of aluminum products by the fifth year, $10 million in 1985, and $13 million the following year. "We always went up and up and up," Greenberg grins, which just could be the underestimation of the decade.

Why such extraordinary growth? Greenberg talks as proudly of the changes he wrought in the industry as he does in the money his firm has made. "When I began, everyone was charging way over what they should have," he bluntly declares. "They were gouging. I was the first who started offering reasonable prices and worked on a marginal profit. I wanted to build up a high volume with extremely good service. From the very start we promised that we would try to be perfect, and would do our very best. And if it's not done properly, we redo it."

In the company's office and showroom are impressive stacks of letters that Greenberg has saved from happy customers. Sixty percent of his business comes from repeats.

"The neighbors have been asking my wife, Margaret, and me how we managed to get such a good-looking job done on our house."—Peter Howell, Toronto.

"The workmen were quiet, efficient, neat, and friendly to a man, and

The staff of Beverley Hills Home Improvements, 1988.

a credit to your company. It's rare in this day and age to be so completely satisfied."—Mrs. Frank O'Leary, Etobicoke.

There have been other strokes of brilliance in the decade-plus history of Beverley Hills Home Improvements. For instance, Greenberg refuses to subcontract, and has his men "work for us and only for us. Our installers can't even work on their own homes without

All work is provided by Beverley Hills craftsmen—no subcontractors. A lot of satisfied customers can attest to the quality of the firm's work policies.

permission!" Indeed, this "strictness" runs throughout the operation. If installers are late, they get fined, and if a call is not returned by a salesperson within 48 hours, there is also a fine. "But the rewards are greater," he says. "Year-round work and better-than-average pay."

Stan Greenberg has no doubts whatsoever why his business has become so successful. "I'm honest and legit, and I know how to handle every possible business situation. It's no secret—just good communications." And, of course, success feeds upon success: "Due to my volume and pricing structure, I can do better than anyone else." He has even taken an idea from the auto industry and put aluminum installing into an assembly line. By having different crews (two on eavestroughs, two on doors, for example), he can do his jobs faster, more efficiently, and with greater customer satisfaction.

Completing more than 60,000 jobs in his first decade, with near-total success rates, comes as no surprise to Stan Greenberg. "I'm a perfectionist," he admits. "I always want better. And look: I'm running a $17-million company with no headaches!"

TRILEA CENTRES INC.

In May 1973 a shopping centre opened in what would soon become the heart of downtown Scarborough, Ontario—Scarborough Town Centre. The location was farmland at the time, with trees and grass all around the centre, and a very old stone farmhouse just a few feet away.

It was an outstanding success from the start, and in retrospect, how could it not be? Within a month the stunning Scarborough Civic Centre opened, with the board of education and city hall within shouting (and shopping) distance. The Borough of Scarborough was rapidly becoming the expanding City of Scarborough, and it had a major, handsome, world-class shopping centre at its very heart.

Back in the early 1970s what was then Trizec Equities Limited joined with Eaton's department store and began to develop this important area, close to the geographical and population centre of Scarborough. Trizec's leadership resulted in Scarborough Town Centre becoming the largest shopping centre in the City of Scarbor-

Scarborough Town Centre, a Trilea Centres Inc. project, is a world-class shopping centre in the heart of downtown Scarborough. The facility covers 1.2 million square feet and features more than 200 stores and services, including Eaton's, Simpsons', and The Bay.

ough and one of the top three suburban shopping centres in Metropolitan Toronto. Indeed, in terms of size and sales, it is among the top five suburban shopping centres in all of Canada.

When it opened in the spring of 1973, it had 135 stores, including two department stores, and covered 850,000 square feet. By 1979 it was expanded by adding a third department store and additional independent stores, making it fully 1.2 million square feet in size.

Today there are more than 200 stores and services in Scarborough Town Centre—an astonishing variety of them—covering every range of price and quality. There are, in fact, 10 cinemas, a full range of restaurants, and a choice of retail shops that are, in the

words of senior vice-president William K. Seli, "all things to all people."

To build such a massive shopping centre today would probably cost in excess of $150 million. There are nearly 6,000 men and women working at the centre, which is open some 70 hours a week. In excess of 200,000 shoppers every six days, or 10 million a year, visit this hub of Scarborough.

And these millions of shoppers average more than $30 per person in purchases (or $55 per actual spender), suggesting just how important a commercial force the centre is to the City of Scarborough. A shopping centre does not average sales in excess of $400 per square foot without considerable support from the community, and it is surprising to note that the average income (and expenditure) of its many shoppers is actually higher than most other shopping centres in Canada. It is surprising because the City of Scarborough has historically projected a blue-collar image, owing to its early beginnings as a suburb of Toronto where one

could find lower-priced "starter" homes.

No longer. The City of Scarborough is generously sprinkled with mansions, as well as some of the loveliest homes in the entire Metropolitan Toronto area, and Scarborough Town Centre has reflected that growing prosperity by featuring dozens of beautiful stores with abundant assortments of timely, quality merchandise.

"We are in the service industry, and we're there to serve the community of Scarborough," says Bill Seli of Trilea matter-of-factly.

But there is nothing at all matter-of-fact about Scarborough Town Centre, which is truly the commercial hub of the entire city. The centre is open from 9:30 a.m. to 9:30 p.m. every Monday through Friday throughout the year, and 9:30 a.m. to 6 p.m. every Saturday, and 10 million shoppers a year—many of whom just hop off the new Scarborough Rapid Transit, and/or work in the many office towers, civic buildings, and homes in the immediate area—can't be wrong.

Canadians knowledgeable of this country's shopping centre history will not be surprised to discover that the

company behind Scarborough Town Centre was and is one of the masters of commercial retail development: Trizec. In 1986 Trilea Centres Inc. was formed, arising from the consolidation that year of the shopping centre interests of Trizec Corporation Ltd. of Calgary and Bramalea Limited of Toronto. It was clearly an amalgamation made in heaven, since the new company now owns and operates 29 shopping centres in more than a dozen cities, all the way from Vancouver in the West to Halifax in the East.

The book value of assets of Trilea Centres Inc. is $1.4 billion (at the time of this writing, in late 1987, but they are expanding all the time). Trilea's shopping centres total more than 13 million square feet of rentable area. And when one considers the brief history of Scarborough Town Centre, one realizes just how inspired this company is.

HERITY GROUP OF COMPANIES

Throughout the decade of the 1980s, during Scarborough's most spectacular period of residential and commercial growth, the Equity Development Group and Heron Homes have been important contributors to what is desirable, memorable, and enduring about this community.

Equity and the well-known residential builder Heron Homes are members of the Herity Group of Companies. As developers and as home builders, they have established a reputation for careful market analysis and a long-term commitment to quality.

The Heathwood, developed by Equity and built by Heron Homes in the early 1980s, is Scarborough's largest planned community of single-family homes. The neighborhood of more than 600 luxury single-family homes led the marketplace in its attention to detail. From parkland and streetscape to the fittings and finishes of the homes themselves, The Heathwood became

"The Park House" was donated by Herity to the City of Scarborough to be used as a public facility. The house and its accompanying playground were put into place before the shovel was placed in the ground to build homes. Equity and Heron continue to prove their ongoing commitment to building communities for residents.

the standard to which family-oriented communities compare.

The Consilium, the complex of gleaming office towers in the commercial heart of Scarborough, was launched by Equity as a forerunner in the provision of first-class urban-core office amenities to Scarborough.

From its state-of-the-art building services to its unique development in conjunction with—rather than in advance of—rapid transit linkage, The Consilium is the model for prestige office facilities in the heart of the city.

Most recently, Equity and Heron Homes have again applied their extensive experience and keen appreciation for the distinctive landmark with the development and construction of The Villages of Abbey Lane.

In its first phase, Herity took an amenities-first approach to developing The Villages of Abbey Lane as an executive community that was unprecedented in scope.

The Villages of Abbey Lane offers a unique neighborhood character, with its quiet cul-de-sacs and winding avenues, its detailed wrought-iron fences separating Abbey Lane's park from the street, and its inviting brick entrance gates setting off Abbey Lane as a community of distinction.

In place before the first family moved in were the community facilities, ranging from fully equipped playground and tennis courts to its own community centre, the 3,500-square-foot Abbey Lane Park House.

The Park House was designed as an enduring structure, though it served at first as the sales pavilion for Heron

Homes, builder of most of the homes of The Villages of Abbey Lane community. On completion of home sales, it was donated to Scarborough by Herity for use as a public facility for the local community. Designed with that enduring purpose in mind, it showcased in its own construction the attention to detail that characterized these exquisite Heron Homes, with all-brick facades, Marley roof tiles, and brass hardware.

As a fully realized community, The Villages of Abbey Lane will have more than its playground and tennis courts, its walkways and open green spaces. As with any village, it will have its own gathering place, in a shopping centre as distinctive as the residential community itself.

Architecturally married to the fine Heron residences, the Abbey Lane Shopping Centre, too, will feature distinctive Marley roof tiles and brick facades along with extensive landscaping. Located across the street from the Park House, the Abbey Lane Shopping Centre is a place to congregate—to socialize as well as to shop.

A mixed-use development, the shopping centre has an autocentre and

The twin towers of the Consilium, linked by an elegant atrium, are a striking landmark at Scarborough's City Centre.

an exclusive group of offices as well as its grocery and boutique shopping facilities.

True to its village inspiration, it features a classic clock tower, as well as its entrance gates, medians, and old-fashioned lighting.

Beneath the imposing clock tower is the centre's unique landscaped sculpture garden, designed by local artists and co-sponsored with Arts Scarborough. At the busiest point in the centre's walkway system, the sculpture garden is intended as much more than a remote artistic monument. An important design criteria was the sculptures' human scale, particularly its "climbability" for the children of Abbey Lane.

As such, the sculpture embraces many of the elements that have made the Herity Group such an important contributor to the future of Scarborough. Like the homes and offices conceived at Herity, it is beautiful both in form and in setting, judged the best of its kind both by professionals and by the families of its community.

The architecture of the Abbey Lane Shopping Centre, with its classic clock tower and sculpture garden, complements the architecture of the luxurious Heron Homes and entrance gates to The Villages of Abbey Lane.

RUNNYMEDE DEVELOPMENT CORPORATION LIMITED

Runnymede Development Corporation Limited is known from Mississauga (to the west of Metro Toronto) to Oshawa (to the east) as one of the most reliable, experienced, trustworthy names in homes, communities, and business parks, and one of Metropolitan Toronto's largest land development and construction companies. What is less known, perhaps, is the colorful history of its remarkable president, Joe Tanenbaum, who, now in his eighties, is still running the thriving firm.

The business was begun by Tanenbaum and a brother back in 1923 as a steel fabrication and bridge building company, putting up such major works as the Burlington Skyway in Hamilton, and the Gardiner Expressway along the Toronto waterfront.

That initial firm was Runnymede Steel Construction Limited. From that very promising beginning evolved Runnymede Development, which has been developing both residential and business communities for several decades, as well as constructing homes, industrial buildings, and shopping centres.

"We pride ourselves on not just building a home, but providing a community environment," declares the company's executive vice-president, Louis I. Greenbaum, with enthusiasm. And the enthusiasm is justified, since the possibilities (and the realization of them) have always been so great: The Runnymede portfolio has included as many as 4,200 acres across the greater Metropolitan Toronto area, since Mr. Tanenbaum was wise enough to begin purchasing land as early as before the war.

From its very start Runnymede has built both wisely and well. (The homes are sold, of course, but the shopping centres are built to be retained; industrial buildings are either leased or sold.) The names of Runnymede's creations have become standards across Metropolitan Toronto: Spring Farm Community in Thornhill, with 2,000 units (and including the award-winning Spring Farm Marketplace), and the Glendale Community, in the town of Pickering, with 1,500 homes.

Scarborough as well has been the recipient of Runnymede's excellence, including such major projects as Burrow's Mill (both residential and industrial); Victoria Crossing, a single-family project; and, most recently, the 89-acre Malvern Heights Business Park.

"Because of our size," notes Greenbaum, "we can include a number of amenities to complement the homes we build, such as good parkland, school sites, and shopping centres. We don't develop merely a few dozen lots, but up to 100 acres and more."

Through 1988 and beyond Runnymede expects to produce as much as one million square feet each year in industrial and commercial space. And those plans—along with Tanenbaum's generous support of hospitals and various social and cultural organizations throughout the City of Scarborough and beyond—only emphasize the importance that Runnymede Development Corporation Limited places on its relationship with the community.

Standing in front of the Runnymede corporate offices are (from left) Bill Swaisland, manager, Industrial Division; Louis Greenbaum, executive vice-president; Joseph Tanenbaum, president; and Patrick Bradley, general counsel and vice-president/ Industrial Division.

ROYAL LEPAGE REAL ESTATE SERVICES LTD.

One of Royal LePage Real Estate Services' offices at 898 Markham Road in Scarborough.

To many people who wish to buy or sell their home (whether in Halifax, Vancouver, or Scarborough), most real estate brokers seem interchangeable. But Royal LePage, the third-largest real estate brokerage firm in Canada and the second largest in the world, has been working determinedly to prove itself different— better.

Most Canadians since early in this century (1913) have thought of A.E. LePage when they thought of real estate brokers. Since December 21, 1984, that long-lasting and highly respected firm has had an important new identity; it was on that day that it merged with the real estate services of Royal Trust, whose own history went all the way back to 1892. Mergers are more frequent than TV commercials, and often just as unappetizing for both customer and shareholder alike. Not so in this case: The establishment of Royal LePage created a new, important real estate company with such assets, staff, and excitement as has rarely been seen in that industry.

Nationally there are more than 10,000 employees of the firm, in all 10 provinces, with 80 percent of them sales people in both residential and non-residential real estate. With close to 400 offices by the end of 1988 (there were 375 in mid-1987), the company continues to grow and thrive. Indeed, it went public on the various stock markets of Canada in 1987, allowing tens of thousands of other Canadians to share in its success.

"The merger allowed the new company to develop and provide a great number of services to the public," declares Royal LePage's vice-president and regional manager, Kenneth Belcher. "Since 1984 it has the support and wherewithal to do all these impressive new things."

For one, Royal LePage was the first to come up with a preapproved mortgage, which it has offered since the fall of 1985. For the first time in history a client could be guaranteed a mortgage even before a house is chosen. Its Home Marketing Program "answers the greatest single complaint in real estate": agents failing to keep in touch with sellers of homes about the marketplace, response to ads, etc.

Royal LePage also has its own, in-house computer system, known as Info-Home, which is independent of the Toronto Real Estate Board's computer, providing information on its listings to brokers across the country. As Belcher puts it, "A buyer can put his requirements into a computer in Edmonton, and he will get information on all Royal LePage listings in the Toronto area in his category."

Pretty smart. But then Royal LePage has always been smartly represented in the City of Scarborough. In mid-1987 there were 10 branch offices in the city; the end of 1989 will probably find 14, covering all four borders of the widespread city. Close to 300 sales people, managers, and support staff work and thrive in Scarborough's Royal LePage branches.

Royal LePage in Scarborough— and in hundreds of other Canadian cities and communities from coast to coast—are out to prove that there is a difference in real estate companies.

LEBOVIC ENTERPRISES LIMITED

Prestige Business Park—450,000 square feet of industrial, commercial, and office space at Finch and Middlefield Avenue in Scarborough.

The 400,000-square-foot West Hill Industrial Park is occupied by tenants such as AICAN, A&W, J.B. Rolland, Max Factor, and Warner Lambert.

Joe and Wolf Lebovic and their father had built the first subdivision in Scarborough all the way back in 1953, when the city had more cows than houses. But Joe's recollections of how and why the family got into the business is the stuff of shaggy-dog stories.

"It was evolutionary," smiles Joe Lebovic. "We were in lumber in Eastern Europe, and came to Canada in 1949. We soon had sawmills in northern Ontario, selling lumber to wholesalers, until we decided that it was the wholesalers who were making all the money. So we sold our mills and opened a lumberyard in Scarborough, selling to builders. But it seemed like they were making the money, so we sold our yard and began to build homes. Then we saw that it was the subdividers who were making the money. So we started developing subdivisions . . ."

And they are still doing it—and very successfully—more than a third of a century later. Lebovic, Sr., retired in 1958 and sold his shares to his two sons, who eventually developed and built everything from houses to condominiums to commercial and industrial properties, stretching from Scarborough to Pickering, Ajax to Aurora. "I look after the subdivisions, industrial and commercial," notes Joe, "while Wolf handles condominiums and housing construction."

The division of labor obviously works, since Lebovic Enterprises Limited is the largest industrial builder in Scarborough, and the largest developer in Scarborough. And the firm has won such revered prizes as the Urban Design Award of 1982, presented by the Borough of Scarborough in honor of a stunning condominium project.

Today more than one million square feet of buildings in Scarborough are built, owned, operated, and managed by Lebovic, and the firm has an additional million square feet that it plans to develop. "We've developed more subdivisions in Scarborough than anyone else," Joe is proud to say, "and we have plans to become the largest custom-built home developer in the city." Lebovic is now building homes in Scarborough and points north and east of Toronto.

The Prestige Business Park at Finch and Middlefield, consisting of 40 acres of offices and industry totalling 400,000 square feet, is a Lebovic project, as is the $56-million industrial shopping development planned at Markham and Finch.

Joe sits on the board of governors of Centenary Hospital, is on the board of directors of Bramalea Ltd., has served on the Scarborough Board of Health, and is a past president of the Urban Development Institute.

"Our homes have a following," declares Wolf Lebovic. "Many people move from one Lebovic home to another, knowing that they will experience quality construction and design."

And the fact that the company retains ownership of all its industrial and shopping centres only underlines the genius behind Lebovic Enterprises Limited: If you build excellence, you can have no fear of being a landlord.

Wilcroft Mews is a complex of 104 townhouses and four single-family homes built and developed at Kennedy and Sheppard by Lebovic Enterprises Limited.

Camargue II and III contain 440 condominium apartments and a shopping plaza featuring IGA, Mac's, Bank of Commerce, and medical and professional suites.

Photo by Glen Jones

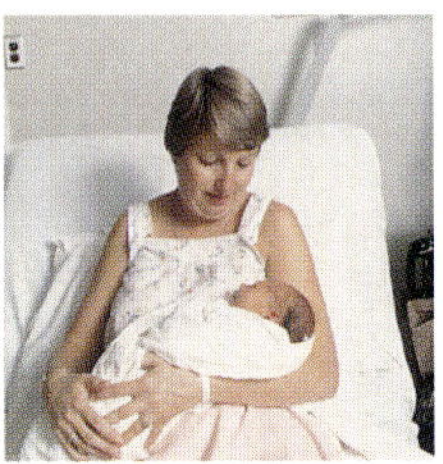

Centenary Hospital, 160-161

E. Scarborough Boys' and Girls' Club, 162

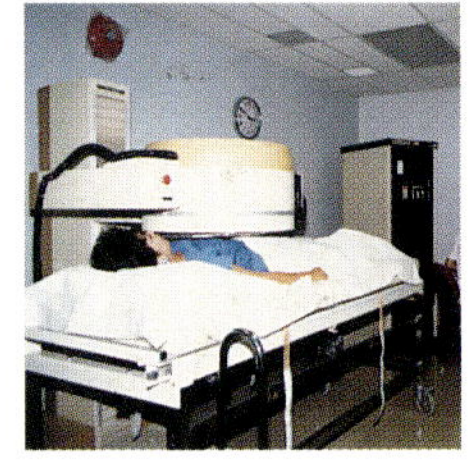

Med-Chem Laboratories Limited, 163

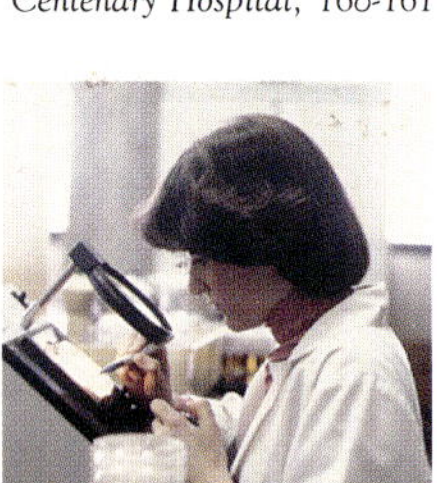

Centennial College, 164

Scarborough Grace General Hospital, 165

QUALITY OF LIFE

Medical and educational institutions and youth organizations contribute to the quality of life of Scarborough area residents.

Residents enjoy Sunday afternoon concerts at the Civic Centre. Courtesy, City of Scarborough

CENTENARY HOSPITAL

Since its beginnings in 1967 the highly respected Centenary Hospital has become a worthy, integral part of the City of Scarborough. This book has already looked at—and applauded—its superior health care, as suggested by many of its new and expanded services.

Today Centenary is an ultra-modern hospital, offering acute care, continuing care, and rehabilitation services. It is committed to the provision of a full range of services in medicine, obstetrics, pediatrics, psychiatry, and surgery, as well as in critical, emergency, ambulatory, and pastoral care.

As a community hospital, Centenary has responded to the needs of the local population by opening the hospital's beautiful new $30-million Margaret Birch Wing in 1986.

Centenary will not rest, however, on the laurels of its 20-year history. This major health care centre will continue to carry out a unique role in the future provision of health care to the City of Scarborough and environs. The future includes caring for patients in an environment that melds new technological sophistication and clinical expertise with a warm, caring attitude, and attention to the emotional needs of the individual.

Keeping in mind the needs of the total person, Centenary became the first hospital in the Metropolitan Toronto area to provide a permanent canine companion for geriatric patients with its recently inaugurated pet therapy program. Pets are important in providing simple companionship—even a sense of purpose and desire to go on living—for the elderly. As volumes of studies have shown, pets give unconditional love, regardless of the age and physical and mental capabilities of the owner or friend. And what you may not know is that playing with a pet, even talking to it, can reduce blood pressure.

Centenary Hospital—a scenic view from the south (left).

Wizard, a golden retriever, conducts rounds as part of the hospital's new pet therapy program (below).

Pet therapy is but one of a variety of programs offered through Centenary's Continuing Care, which makes up current and future plans to meet the growing demands of an aging population. Respite care, admission of up to one month for men and women with long-term illnesses, provides relief for their caregivers, as well as a thorough physical assessment of the patient. The program works toward the patients returning home more confident and self-reliant.

Centenary is also planning to take a leadership role in the field of health-related women's issues. Nearly $1.5 million of the hospital's expansion project was directed toward its maternity, nursery, and gynecology services—only the first step in an extensive and enthusiastic plan that includes a birthing centre, and more clinical and educational programs for women.

In fact, Centenary plans to provide more ongoing programs to help Scarborough residents stay healthy and out of hospital. A Smoke Stoppers program and Diabetes Education Centre have already begun, with future plans aimed at nutrition, fitness, stress management, and other health concerns.

A $10-million, health-related shopping mall and medical office building is planned for 1989 to further accommodate consumer needs. It will provide one-stop shopping access to medical supplies, life-style services, doctors' offices, and the hospital. It is the first project of this scale to be initiated by a community hospital in Canada.

Like most first-class health care institutions, Centenary relies on its vibrant volunteers to help support many of its planned and existing patient services. The Auxiliary, with more than 450 adults and another 100 teens and student aides, provides every service from television rentals to baby photographs, flower delivery, the library cart service, and the Post-Operative Information Centre. Since its inception in 1965 the Auxiliary has donated in excess of $3.8 million to Centenary through its services and special fund-raising events. The Auxiliary truly lives up to its reputation as "people who care."

In fact, it is because of the people who make up Centenary Hospital—its staff, physicians, and volunteers—that the institution has achieved such a superb reputation in the field of community health, and it deserves all the praise and support that it gets.

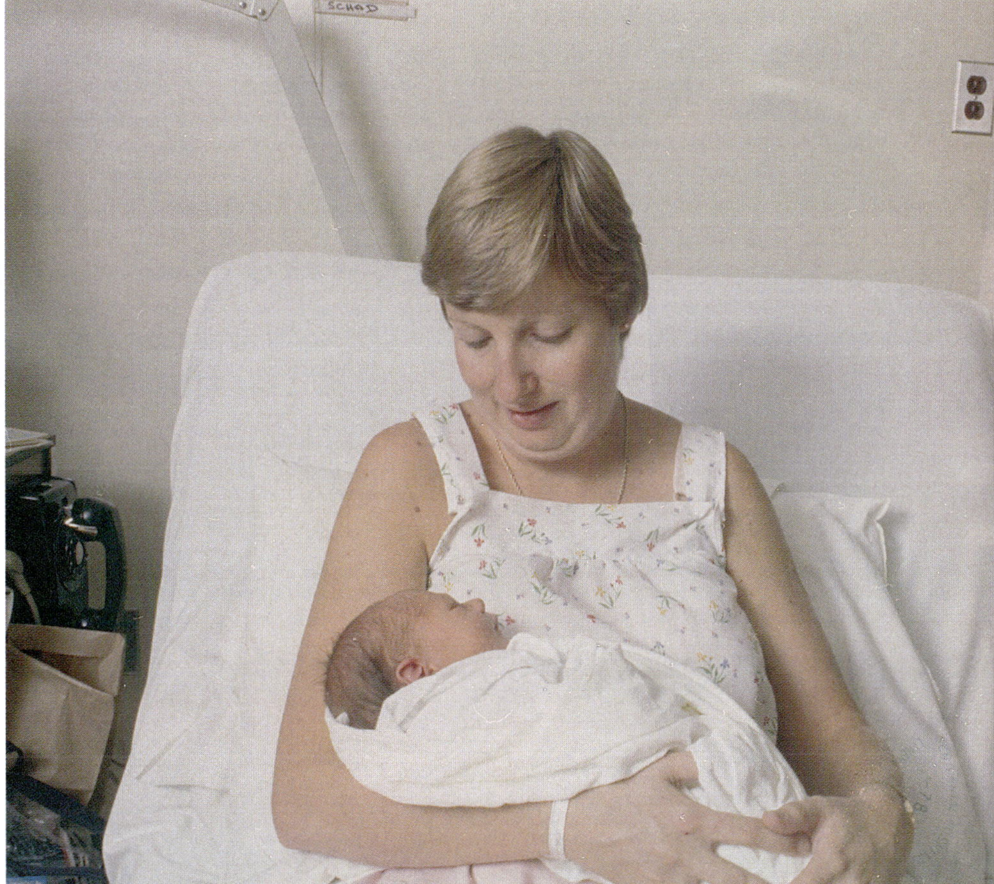

Recent renovations to Centenary's maternity, nursery, and gynecology units enables the hospital to cater to the needs of women. Close to 2,800 babies are born there annually.

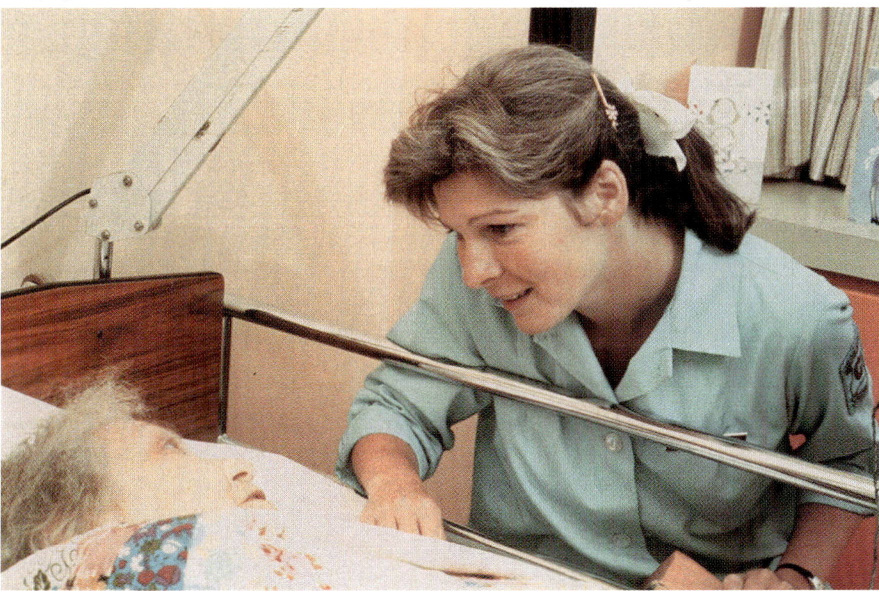

More than 500 volunteers live up to their reputation as "people who care."

EAST SCARBOROUGH BOYS' AND GIRLS' CLUB

In a society that prides itself on its ability to cross vast distances at greater and greater speeds, and to process information and products at an almost astronomical pace, often the smaller, quieter elements of our society are overlooked: the children.

The East Scarborough Boys' and Girls' Club is a nonprofit organization that attempts to provide children and youth with a sense of belonging and well-being. The club reflects the many cultural faces of Canadian society, and believes welcoming and embracing multiculturalism will give all participants a sense of belonging in a world society.

In providing a caring environment, the club attempts to develop with the children and youth a sense of self-esteem, competency, and self-belief—the cornerstones of growth and learning.

expanding services to the community.

The East Scarborough Boys' and Girls' Club is supported by the United Way, Metro Community Social Services, and the City of Scarborough. With all its giving members and participants, and all the services it provides, the East Scarborough Boys' and Girls' Club is a community treasure.

The club relies on the dynamics of its participants, volunteers, and staff. The programs are most often run by talented individuals who volunteer their time and experience for the children. Jazz, judo, and ceramics are but a few of the courses offered through the club.

During the summer months the day camp (offered for children between the ages of 6 and 12), is popular with both parents and children. It is often their first introduction to the East Scarborough Boys' and Girls' Club. The

Parent/Child Centre works in a similar fashion, introducing families to the club while providing a place and a means by which young children and their parents are given the opportunity to meet their neighbors. The teens are a dynamic group. Their interaction usually takes the form of dances, fundraising campaigns, and wilderness camping trips.

The East Scarborough Boys' and Girls' Club, as a nonprofit organization, relies greatly on the generosity of the community and small businesses. Such generosity has taken the form of this profile, which allows the club to relay its mission to an even greater public.

This profile was sponsored by Don Taylor, president of the Riser Group, an impressive organization in its own right.

Today Riser is one of the largest installers of computer and communication systems in Canada. Taylor began his business in 1981, and since then sales have grown to $10 million with 120 employees.

Don Taylor and the Riser Group place a great emphasis on quality and services, and it is to this he attributes his success. Although Riser's president proudly predicts that by 1992 the Riser Group will be a $30-million business, one senses he, as the president since 1985, is just as proud of his involvement with the East Scarborough Boys' and Girls' Club.

The East Scarborough Boys' and Girls' Club embraces children of the many cultures in Canadian society. The club strives to provide its young participants with a sense of well-being and self-esteem.

For two decades the East Scarborough Boys' and Girls' Club has been providing much-needed, quality services for the community's children. More than 650 individuals, ranging from tots to teens, utilize the club's facilities and programs.

Through the efforts of volunteers on the board and committees, the club was able to raise funds in excess of one million dollars, enabling it to house itself in facilities that could grow with its

MED-CHEM LABORATORIES LIMITED

The City of Scarborough boasts of a very successful, reliable, and highly respected firm, Med-Chem Laboratories Limited, which has been providing services to doctors and hospitals since it opened its first office on Sheppard Avenue East in April 1970.

When Med-Chem first began there were two employees performing basic biochemistry, hematology, microbiology, and electrocardiograms. Today there are more than 500 employees, ranging from medical technologists through support staff, covering everything from collecting specimens to data entry, specimen testing, and result reporting. Indeed, the 22 collection centres across Metro Toronto and beyond make Med-Chem the second-largest reference lab in the province and the second-largest laboratory overall in Ontario—all this growth in less than two decades!

Med-Chem Laboratories Limited is a private company, but its services could not be more in the public interest, as can be seen by its statistics: Its laboratories do the testing on more than 4,000 patients per day, who provide roughly 20,000 specimens seven days a week.

The reliability of the firm can be attested to by one simple fact— Med-Chem is the only laboratory that does the testing for all in-vitro fertilization (commonly called test-tube babies) in Metropolitan Toronto. This

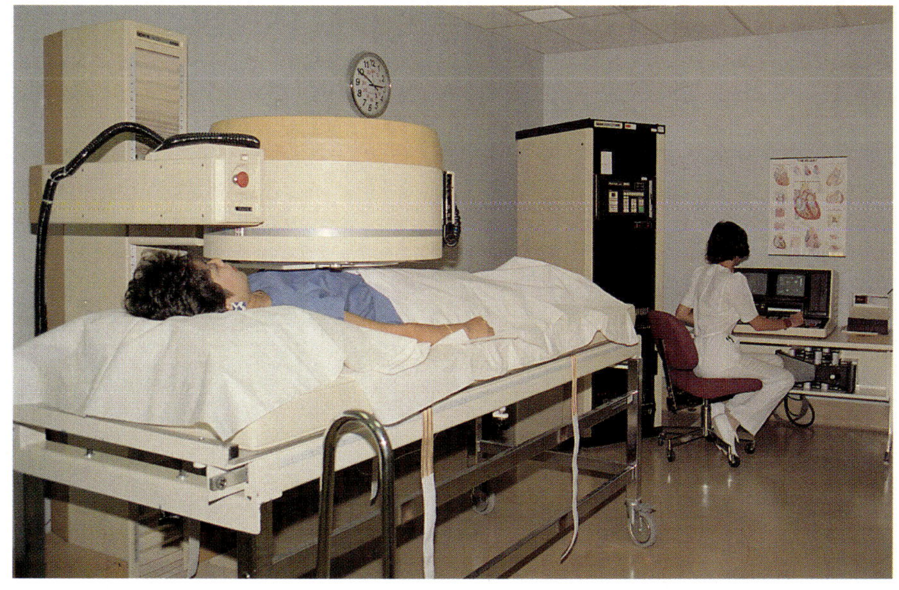

program is known as the Life Program, and that is precisely what it achieves, better than 30 percent of the time.

Two of the four founders from 1970 are still with the firm—Gora Aditya, its president, and Dr. Rodney Ellis, its vice-president/science and technology. The affection displayed among the employees and toward the administration is echoed in the treatment of the tens of thousands of patients being tested. "We pride ourselves on our care, from the person who takes the blood sample through to the computer analysis. Our motto is

Quality, Care, and Service, and we never forget it," states Linda Ford.

That same care is reflected in the policy of participative management, originating from Med-Chem's president, Gora Aditya, and filtering down throughout the company to each and every employee. The firm's own Fitness Centre instituted within the building encourages that same participation and is enthusiastically supported by the employees, whether it be through badminton games, fitness classes, walking, mini-golf, or Tai-chi.

Med-Chem Laboratories has moved three times, each time to a larger building on the same street, Sheppard Avenue East, in Scarborough. Its fourth move took place in 1988, once again on Sheppard Avenue East.

Med-Chem Laboratories Limited did not become the largest laboratory in Scarborough without innovations. From customer service to refrigerated cars, from state-of-the-art equipment to full computerization, the firm has been experiencing rapid growth each year for the past half-decade. Quality control, efficiency, and patient care all have contributed to make Med-Chem one of the major names in laboratory testing. After all, its employees know that lives truly do depend on them.

CENTENNIAL COLLEGE

In a recent advertisement in several major Toronto newspapers, Centennial College was plugging one of its unique programs. The ad noted, "Book and magazine publishing is the only full-time program of its kind in Canada . . . At Centennial College, you'll be involved in editing, marketing, and design of books and magazines from cover to cover."

Then the ad quotes *Quill & Quire* magazine, a major periodical about publishing in Canada: ". . . graduates of a publishing course offered by Centennial probably have a more thorough knowledge of publishing than a lot of their prospective employers."

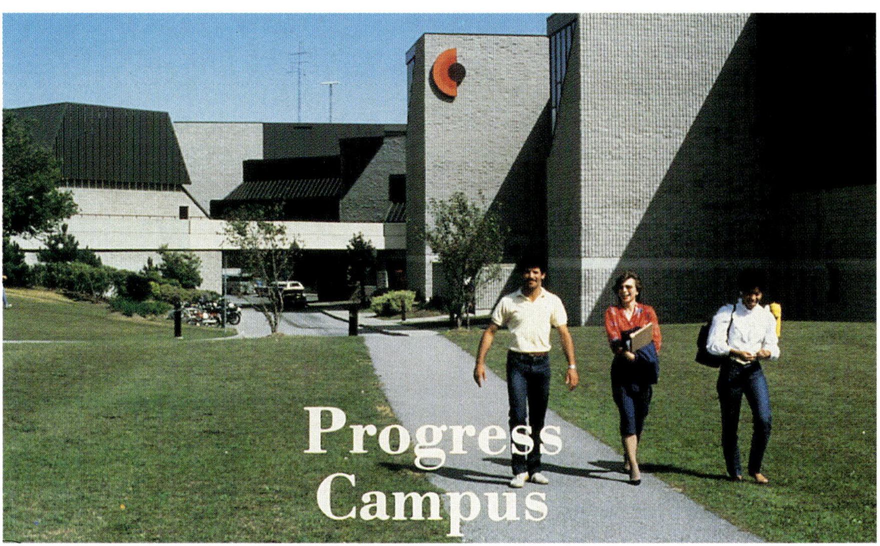

Centennial's Progress Campus houses the schools of business and engineering technology.

The computer-assisted design labs are booked 24 hours a day, seven days a week.

It's true. And it is facts such as these, surprising as they may be to prospective employers, that make the college one of the gems of Ontario's—and Canada's—postsecondary institutions.

The president of Centennial, Bev McCauley, does not see his institution as merely a major Ontario college. "If Canada wants to compete internationally, then institutions such as Centennial must be seen as equal partners with business, industry, and government, to meet future challenges."

McCauley talks proudly of the institution he has headed since 1978. He's excited about the college's Alternate Fuel Centre, its Composites Innovation Centre, its always-overflowing CAD labs (computer-assisted design), and the many classrooms needed year round to satisfy the hundreds clamouring for real estate licences. "We don't want to sit back and rest on our laurels," he cautions. "We have to continue to meet new opportunities as one of Ontario's growth industries."

Biotechnology is just one of Centennial's many unique programs.

Centennial has three campuses in Scarborough—including Progress Campus, nearly 50 acres in size. A $10.3-million addition is scheduled for completion in September 1989. He recalls joining the college in the summer of 1967 to start up a part-time studies area. By that September there were 500 part-time students, and he believed that "if we got 1,000, we'd have reached our goal." Today there are 50,000 part-time and 10,000 full-time learners at four campuses in Scarborough and East York.

McCauley realizes that Centennial College is on the leading edge. "The rapid technological changes taking place mean companies must update their employees," he says. Then he adds thoughtfully, "Before 1967 where did people go?" Today the answer is clear—Centennial College.

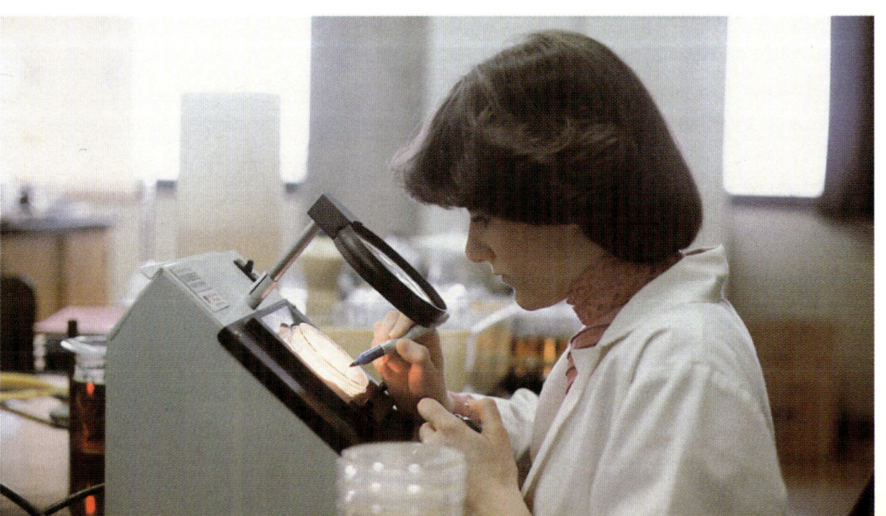

SCARBOROUGH GRACE GENERAL HOSPITAL

Letters from former patients reflect something of the compassionate care being provided by Scarborough's newest hospital, the Scarborough Grace.

"I cannot adequately express the genuine gratitude that I feel toward your staff . . . I admire their close attention to detail, and I feel that they truly care about their patients . . ."

"I just spent five days at Scarborough Grace Hospital, and I am writing to say how very pleased and impressed I was . . ."

But while all the letters are much appreciated, they hardly come as a surprise. For the Salvation Army has been in hospital work for nearly a century, and Major Harold Thornhill, the Grace's executive director, has been working in the hospital field for nearly three decades.

"It began back in the late nineteenth century in India, when a young Salvation Army officer saw the need for medical care among the poor, and began a small dispensary," says Thornhill. In Canada, Salvation Army hospitals have been prominent since the first was incorporated in Winnipeg back in 1904. Today they number 11, stretching from St. John's, Newfoundland, in the East to Vancouver in the West.

And newest, of course, is Scarborough Grace, located wisely on Birchmount Avenue, "where studies by the Toronto Hospital Planning Council showed a new hospital would be required." Both of the other Scarborough hospitals are located below the major dividing line of Highway 401, creating "a psychological boundary," Thornhill points out.

In its first few years of existence Scarborough Grace already has more than 800 full-time employees, and some 200 more part-time workers. Also on staff are in excess of 200 private medical practitioners. And the attractive hospital is already "looking at the demographic growth of the area," and is considering adding another floor—meaning more than 150 additional beds—by the early part of the 1990s.

The emphasis at Scarborough Grace is, of course, "treating the whole person, considering not only the patient's medical needs, but the social, emotional, and spiritual ones as well. In-

Scarborough Grace General Hospital, the city's newest community general hospital, is committed to caring for the whole person.

Prenatal, obstetrical, and postpartum care are areas of particular strength at Scarborough Grace General Hospital.

deed, the Salvation Army hospitals had chaplains available many decades before other medical institutions did, always ready to connect patients with their own religious pastor in times of need.

"We are providing the majority of the medical and hospital services needed by the community," declares Thornhill, "so the residents needn't go elsewhere in Scarborough or outside the city for most of their care." The hospital's special expertise, he believes, is rapidly becoming obstetrics, "in which Salvation Army hospitals have always been in the forefront."

So, too, with Scarborough Grace General Hospital, which admitted its first patients as recently as November 1985, and has already become an integral part of the City of Scarborough.

Honda Canada Inc.,.
168-169

The Guild Inn, 170-171

Welcome Wagon Ltd.,
172-173

Foster Pontiac Buick Ltd.,
174

Hogan Chevrolet-Oldsmobile
Ltd., 175

Cross-Canada Car Leasing
Ltd., 176

Henley Chemicals Ltd., 177

Volkswagen Canada Inc.,
178

Bick's Pickles, 179

Golden Mile Motors Ltd./
Scarborough Toyota/Nissan,
180

Toyota Canada Inc., 181

Midas Canada Incorpo-
rated, 182

Marvin Starr Pontiac Buick
Inc., 183

Minolta Business Equipment
(Canada) Ltd., 184

CHAPTER SEVENTEEN

THE MARKETPLACE

The area's retail establishments, service industries, and products are enjoyed by residents and visitors to the area.

Part of the City Centre, Town Centre consists of over 200 stores and eating establishments. Photo by Glen Jones

HONDA CANADA INC.

"From little acorns mighty oaks grow," reads the old proverb. In the very similar case of Honda Canada Inc., the saying might be: "From little motorcycle manufacturers mighty automobile industries grow." For it was only as far back as 1962 that Honda first entered the Canadian market with merely one model of a two-wheel vehicle, the C-240 motorcycle. It retailed for $279, and a mightier acorn was never seen in the North.

Just three years later Honda was selling automobiles in Canada; the first was its S-600 sports roadster, retailing at $2,400, and the rest is history. For nine consecutive years, until 1986, Honda was the number-one imported car in Canada, only briefly bounced by another automobile. Then, in 1987, Honda was back in its usual, proper place in the lead, and for reasons that have been duly noted and published by many well-respected professional sources.

In 1983 the Honda Prelude was voted first, over the VW Scirocco and the Toyota Celica GT-S, in competitive test driving by *Road & Track.* The following year Honda was called the Import Car of the Year by *Motor Trend.* In 1987 Honda was named the Best Built Car in Canada by *World of Wheels.* And, to dispel any fears that the other years may have seen an unsatisfactory product, the Accord was on *Car and Driver*'s 10 Best Built Car list from 1982 through 1987, and Honda automobiles have been bringing in showrooms full of awards for the past dozen years, for quality, performance, reliability, and economy. That's what the automotive experts say about Honda.

It is not by chance that such a wildly successful company chose to first settle, and later to expand, within the expansive borders of Scarborough, Ontario. Honda Canada was originally born in a tiny office on Rolark Drive in the city, just behind where the Ramada Renaissance now stands, and finally settled in its present, generous location of 235,000 square feet on Milner Avenue in 1982. But it was not only due to Scarborough's vastness; it was also Scarborough's excellent work force. Honda officials happily point out that the city has always been "a good source" of employees, and that virtually all of those who work in its beautiful Canadian headquarters are Scarborough residents.

Honda has not forgotten where its vehicular roots are either; within two years after it first came to Canada, Honda accounted for nearly one-half of

The 1988 Accord EXi four-door sedan was co-winner (with its LX stablemate) of the Automotive Association of Canada's "Best Built in Canada in 1987."

all motorcycles sold in this country—a lead the company has maintained ever since. In addition, Honda is a respected name in scooters, all-terrain vehicles, and power equipment products—as well as its superb automobiles.

And what superb automobiles they are, too. The Honda Accord remains the star of the line to the point that Honda invested $200 million in 450 acres of land, building and equipping a major plant in Alliston, Ontario, just an hour northwest of Scarborough. Today the manufacturing plant employs 900, and produced some 15,000 cars (of the 70,000 sold) in 1987.

The Scarborough head office of Honda Canada employs approximately 250 men and women, ranging from national administration to data processing to support staff, as well as warehouse people, who handle parts for all Honda products. (There are parts warehouses in Vancouver and Montreal as well, along with five zone offices, including Halifax and Winnipeg. And they have been computerized since the early days.)

Across Canada there are more than 200 Honda dealers, selling the Civic, the Accord, and the Prelude. They were recently joined by several dozen Acura dealers, also spread across Canada. The total dealer network of Acura dealers is projected to reach 50 by 1989. The concept is quite inspired: Acura dealers will sell only the Legend and the Integra, both upscale and both appealing to a different segment of the market than those who have so eagerly sought out the excellent, yet low-priced Honda Civics and Accords. To put it another way, before the Acura Division began, men and women who usually purchase $20,000-$40,000 automobiles might not have visited a Honda dealer; with the classy new Legends and Integras, they will be attracted to the Acura offerings.

And they should, if they are

The 1988 Acura Legend L coupe, the flagship model of the Acura lineup, is available exclusively at Acura dealerships across Canada. Acura is a division of Honda Canada Inc.

shoppers and acquainted with the way Honda keeps bringing in the accolades. Like this quotation from *Motor Trend* magazine, when Honda beat out the much-higher-priced Audi 5000 S Turbo and Mercedes Benz 190E 2.3: "Honda may very well be the best car company in the world today. Why? Because at Honda product comes before everything else. Technically innovative, imaginative product."

Impressive words, especially from writers who judge all cars equally on their merits. And Honda Canada Inc., as it moves into its second quarter-century of doing business in Canada and Scarborough, continues to zoom forward with the smoothness and speed of, yes, a Honda.

THE GUILD INN

There are many unique places in Canada, from the frozen expanses of the Yukon to the wondrous peaks of the Rocky Mountains. But there is probably no hotel complex in this country—and most likely in the world—that is as unique, as fascinating, and as overflowing with historical and architectural beauty—as well as vacation potential—as The Guild Inn in Scarborough.

The reasons are immediately obvious: Where else in Canada is such a stunning resort sitting on 90 acres less than a half-hour drive from the heart of a major downtown area? The Guild Inn is a remarkable concept, and all the more so because of the brilliant collection of historic architecture and sculpture spread over its expansive grounds.

The Guild Inn has been steadily modernizing over the past few years as

Beautifully landscaped grounds surround the Gibson House gates, which welcome guests to the timelessness of The Guild Inn.

well, so while it has become better able to handle business seminars and conferences like all other major hotels, it is also slanting itself toward activities for families, such as its delightful Treasure Hunt, where guests are challenged to discover particular monuments conserved from some of Toronto's most famous historic buildings, which had long before been torn down and nearly lost to "progress."

The Guild Inn was born back in the depths of the Great Depression, when Rosa and Spencer Clark purchased the magnificent property on the edge of Scarborough Bluffs. There were soon working shops and studios in sculpture, batiks, handloom weaving, ceram-

ics, pewter, and more, leading to a growing number of visitors. Dining facilities and guest rooms were eventually added, so that The Guild of All Arts soon became a flourishing country inn—The Guild Inn, as it would eventually become known.

The war years saw The Guild become an official naval base, but it was returned to the Clarks in 1947. For a number of years it continued on as The Guild of All Arts, until the area was absorbed into Metropolitan Toronto, leading to skyrocketing taxes, and the necessary sale of some 400 of its acres. In 1978 Metropolitan Toronto and the Ontario government purchased The Guild and its surrounding land, with Spencer Clark continuing to operate it, and expanded its fabulous art and historic collections. The Guild Inn has recently been acquired by new management who are committed to developing a unique resort/conference facility while maintaining the existing charm and ambience of the setting.

There are 96 sleeping rooms, a baker's dozen conference rooms, a dining room, and a new garden dining area as of 1988, and there will be even greater changes and improvements taking place in the months and years ahead. It will be a determined "taking the best of the old and adding to it," thereby increasing the phenomenal attractions and attractiveness already present on the generous property.

Still to come in the years ahead are plans for an indoor swimming pool, Jacuzzis, more tennis courts, health programmes, and additional rooms. There will also be the need to expand the food and beverage facilities, recreational facilities, and staff. All of these are pieces that must be put together, and will be because of the determination of The Guild Inn to remain a major tourist attraction, as well as a resort/conference hotel, in the Metropolitan Toronto area.

Many of the pieces are there already, of course, thanks to the Clarks and the good taste that went into The Guild Inn over its half-century-plus of existence. The lovely, generous rooms, for example, each have two double beds. And the six one- and two-bedroom suites all possess balconies and spectacular views.

And what of the numerous other amenities? The Guild Inn is but a two-minute walk from the fabulous Scarborough Bluffs, which have, at their feet, some of the best salmon fishing in the world.

What it comes down to is simple: The amenities and vastness of a resort/conference center, just minutes from downtown Scarborough and Toronto. The sales in April 1987 were some 16 percent over the previous year, and the sales in May were 25 to 30 percent higher than those in May 1986, suggesting that the message is rapidly spreading that The Guild Inn is a delight to rediscover or to experience for the first time.

It remains almost unbelievable: nearly 100 acres of parkland, charming rooms, the awesome Scarborough Bluffs, plus everything from the Stanley Barracks gates (forged in England in 1839 and shipped to Canada for the main military fortification of the newly incorporated City of Toronto) to the Bell and Belfry from Victoria Park School (built in 1873 and demolished in 1964, to make way for Highway 401). And quality food, as well. In-

The well-known green-and-white Guild Inn marquee is framed between some of the ancient columns that grace the grounds.

deed, the most popular item in the house today is its astonishingly delicious, naturally smoked salmon, which is made right at the inn, and sold both as an appetizer and in its lovely gift shop.

The Guild Inn is truly a very special resort/conference hotel. As one of its delighted visitors told this writer, "I've never seen anything like this in the middle of a city!"

But with its highly competitive

The superb cuisine is enhanced by white linen, peach napkins, and a simple but elegant place setting.

room rates and the major modernization and improvements always being planned, tens of thousands of guests will soon be discovering (and more than likely re-discovering) the attractive marriage of "the old and the new" features that The Guild has to offer.

WELCOME WAGON LTD.

Welcome Wagon is known and perceived as help and kindness delivered in person far more than it is perceived as the significant and successful national service company that it has become, with its head office established in Scarborough.

Two years after it was founded in the United States, Welcome Wagon was launched in Canada and expanded during the "dirty thirties" from Vancouver to span the length and breadth of all 10 provinces and the Yukon.

The Welcome Wagon way of presenting data and detail on available public and community services and introducing local merchants and services to new residents in a community provides an important service for them and personalized promotion for the businesses involved.

The Welcome Wagon Hostess and her decorated basket personify the concept of a caring community and local businesses to whom people and service are important. Their gifts, greetings, and invitations, delivered by her, say it tangibly.

The token gifts Welcome Wagon brings are thoughtful and may range from a loaf of bread to a magnetic note holder to a grease job for the car. Local information may include maps, detail of garbage pickup, library location and hours, and health services.

Because the families who are welcomed receive the service without

A proud mother and her little daughter are greeted with gifts, congratulations, and admiration from the Baby Welcome hostess. Photo by Elizabeth Teng

charge or obligation, they and the public at large think of Welcome Wagon as a nonprofit organization. However, an ever-growing sector of the business community is discovering the tremendous value of the direct link that Welcome Wagon provides for them to increase their clientele.

Today more than 1,200 Welcome Wagon Hostesses across Canada work within their local communities—a dozen or more in Scarborough itself. A team of 30 field managers supervise, hire, train, and guide them. From the Scarborough head office, more than 40 employees coordinate the Welcome Wagon administration, which evolves from representing more than 15,000 businesses and visiting with more than 300,000 families individually each year.

Welcome Wagon is automatically associated with the moving process, but the company now serves many other circumstances and occasions. Special events are organized: Bridal Parties for brides-to-be, Baby Showers for expectant mothers, and Plus Sixty Showcases for the retired and semi-retired.

Children look on in anticipation as the Welcome Wagon hostess brings gifts and information to welcome new arrivals into the community. Photo by Elizabeth Teng

and the opportunity awaits others as they earn the privilege of ownership. Since Canadian ownership was achieved in 1979, Welcome Wagon's sales have more than tripled.

Welcome Wagon enjoys the hundreds of unsolicited citations it receives from civic officials and communities in recognition of the many services its Hostesses provide. Mayors even proclaim Welcome Wagon weeks, and newspapers give the organization's efforts a "lot of ink."

Welcome Wagon Ltd. continues to pleasantly surprise hundreds of thousands of people across Canada, to powerfully promote the businesses it represents, and to progressively reward its many hundreds of employees. How can it help but be famous for its service, and how can it help but be recognized as significant and successful in its public relations and promotional capabilities?

Congratulations are brought to the new president of Volkswagen in his Scarborough office by the Executive Welcome Division of Welcome Wagon Ltd. Photo By Elizabeth Teng

Bridal fashions draw keen interest at a Welcome Wagon bridal party. Photo by Elizabeth Teng

New mothers and their babies are visited in hospital or thereafter at home. There is Campus Welcome for the college student at registration, business-to-business presentations for executives and professionals when change and movement occur, and Convention Welcome for visiting delegates. All are designed to bridge the gap between the needs of changing situations and those who can best serve them.

In the summer of 1987 yet another dimension was added to Welcome Wagon with the creation of the Wagon Post Division through which the link with hundreds of thousands of families is continued by mail. A simple example would be that of sending related business information to new parents about solid baby foods several months after the baby's birth, just when the need for it occurs. Growth and expansion are made of such intelligent and logical concepts.

Less than a decade ago Welcome Wagon Ltd. became Canadian owned when a group of Canadian management purchased it outright from the U.S. owners. Since then the number of management shareholders has grown to 18,

FOSTER PONTIAC BUICK LTD.

Foster Pontiac Buick Ltd. is the longest-established new car dealership in Scarborough, and its growth parallels the majestic expansion of the city from a sleepy, rural hamlet to a bustling metropolis.

Bob Foster has an office filled with golf trophies, plaques from the mother corporation, a birdcage with a chirping inhabitant, an hourglass, and—most revered of all—the industry's highest achievement: the *Time* magazine Quality of the Year Award, which not only recognizes business success but a concern with improving the quality of life within the community as well.

His father, Harry J. Foster, purchased five acres of property at Sheppard Avenue near Warden back in 1952, when the today-busy street was a two-lane road. "People were afraid to come in on weekends," Bob recalls, "and we'd have to go up to their bumper-to-bumper cars and just talk to them as they headed out to their summer cottages."

The warmth and enthusiasm worked—as did the father, son, and handful of employees. Back in "the heyday of the 1950s," they were lucky to

The showroom, leasing area , used cars, and general office.

sell 300 cars a year. Today the 90 people on staff sell over 2,300 cars a year, which has more than kept up with inflation.

As in every business there can be trying times. The sudden passing of the firm's founder, Harry J. Foster, shortly after his son Bob became president in 1970, was especially difficult. However, Foster Pontiac Buick has gone a long way since it "once traded a used Ford for a load of gravel needed to cover our driveway." It has gained renown across Scarborough, and many cities beyond, as a reliable, trustworthy, solid member of the business community. "Scarborough has been good to us," Foster says. "We feel it's important to give much back.

"We're known for our reliability," he confesses. "I never tire of people telling me they appreciate the reputation we seem to have earned."

As a man who fought for Canada in World War II, Bob Foster's attitudes toward his employees, as well as the community at large, radiate that same sense of faith and camaraderie. "We're supportive of each other," he says, noting the 18-year-old social club of Foster Pontiac Buick staff members. His recollections of "the generosity of the Salvation Army during the war" led to a steady support of the Agincourt Temple, and free loans of a van to take children to and from Sunday School. Similarly, the three hospitals of Scarborough receive ongoing support.

Indicative of the good relationship the company has with its employees is that the office staff; service, parts, and used car managers; and tune-up mechanics have been associated for an average of close to two decades each.

It is a family-oriented firm. Jeffrey Foster, Bob's son, is now general sales manager—and with the birth of Jesse Robert Foster in the fall of 1986, Foster Pontiac Buick Ltd. could go on forever.

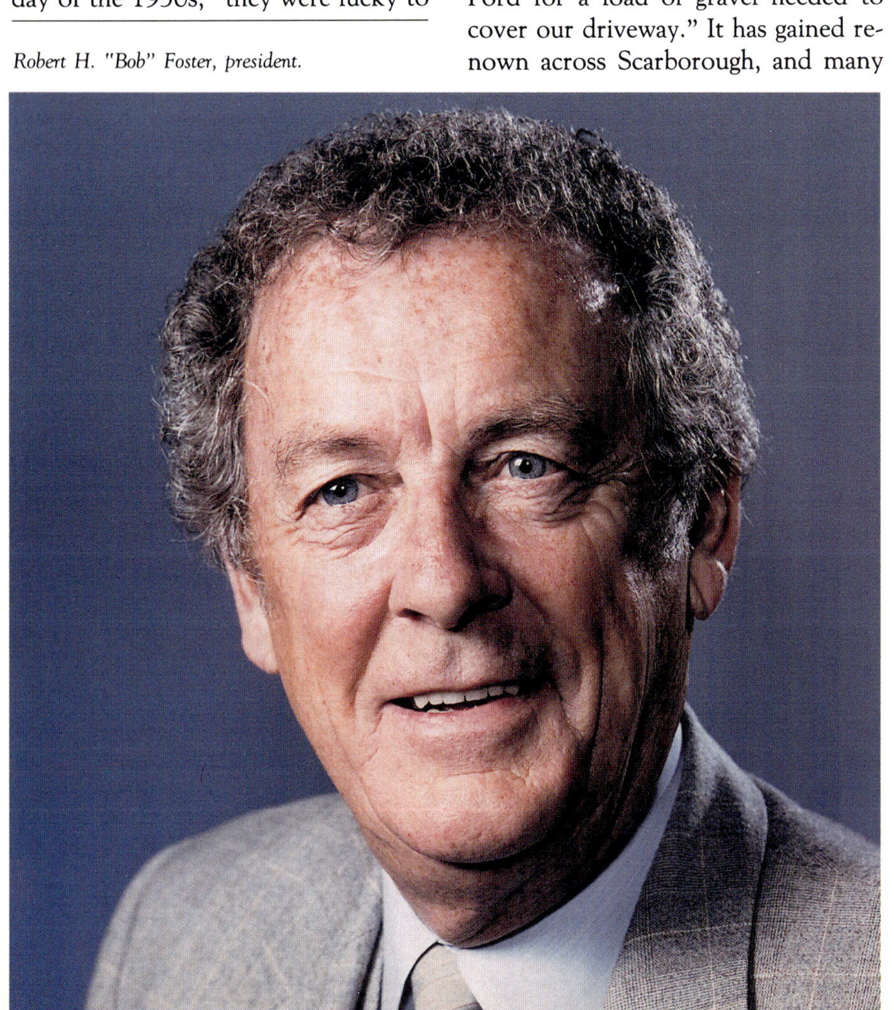

Robert H. "Bob" Foster, president.

HOGAN CHEVROLET-OLDSMOBILE LTD.

Hogan Chevrolet-Oldsmobile is a famous and respected name in General Motors, and in all automotive circles—and it has been such for six full decades. Founded in 1928 by George W. Hogan, Sr., as a Pontiac-Buick dealer on the Danforth, it was taken over by his son in 1955, who ran it until his death in 1965. Then Grant G. Brown took over for a decade, before selling it to its fourth president in 1977.

Ralph Phillips may not have been with Hogan from its start—although he did work for General Motors for 17 years, starting in the sales department of its Oshawa office and eventually becoming business manager of its Toronto zone—but he is most assuredly a man with a vision.

He, along with his partners, T.A. Karrys and T.C. Potma, moved the firm to Scarborough in 1980, changing its automobile line to Chevrolet and Oldsmobile but keeping that long-admired name. "It was a good location, at 5000 Sheppard Avenue East, and we found six acres here. We wanted to retain our old customers, and we've now developed considerable local business as well."

It was residential and agricultural just a few years ago, but both Phillips and General Motors realized that the northeast section of Scarborough was

Under the leadership of R.C. Phillips, Hogan Chevrolet-Oldsmobile Ltd. opened in Scarborough in 1980 at 5000 Sheppard Avenue East.

the fastest-growing area of Metropolitan Toronto. And how right they were: The 85 employees in 1980 have now nearly doubled, to more than 150, and the figure of 1,100 cars sold in its first year in Scarborough is now exceeding 2,000 (and add a further 1,000 used cars to that number).

Today Hogan is the largest Chevrolet-Oldsmobile dealer in the City of Scarborough. "They are very popular cars," says Phillips.

A very innovative and concerned employer, Ralph Phillips established an extensive profit-sharing program to make his growing number of employees a part of his firm's success. He has also developed a highly computerized shop. "We are a service-minded dealership that believes the customer is king" is his motto.

And most visionary of all is Phillips' concept of an Auto Mall. His company owns 42 acres just three miles due east of Hogan, along Sheppard, where he plans a fully serviced auto shopping mall. It will have several dealerships, an accompanying office complex, even an automobile science centre.

"If we can pull it off, it'll be one of the best auto malls in North America," Phillips claims. He owns a General Motors dealership with a proud name that extends back to the 1920s, and a new development that will reach forward into the next century. And the 55-years-of-service employee who passed away in 1983 merely underlines the fact: Hogan Chevrolet-Oldsmobile Ltd., and the soon-to-come Auto Mall, are visions of both the past and the future—both growing majestically in Scarborough.

R.C. Phillips, president.

CROSS-CANADA CAR LEASING LTD.

More than 35 years ago, in 1952, only a few auto leasing companies operated in Canada. This was a new industry. Only Cross-Canada Car Leasing Ltd. continues to thrive at its Scarborough head office, and all the way across this very large country. "We're the oldest leasing company in Canada," claims the founder and present chairman, Grover C. Robertson. And, with more than 3,000 vehicles leased predominantly to firms in all 10 provinces, and $20 million-plus in annual billings as of mid-1988, it is one of the most impressive as well.

Cross-Canada has always been in Toronto's east end and, since 1971, on Kennedy Road, not far from the 401—and just minutes from the Scarborough City Hall and the Town Centre. There are also offices and vehicle service centres in Mississauga, near the Toronto airport, and in Saint-Laurent (Montreal) Quebec; but in the world of leasing, the key is service.

That is why the business has a network of associated dealers and service outlets across Canada—"from Victoria, British Columbia, to Gander, Newfoundland" in the words of president Bill Gow. What this means is "if your car breaks down in Lethbridge, Alberta, a dealer will take care of everything, and send the bill off to Cross-Canada's Scarborough office. This unique plan is Full Maintenance Leasing."

G.C. Robertson, chairman of Cross-Canada Car Leasing Ltd., founded the company in 1952.

That is the point of leasing, is it not? The tax breaks are fine, and money savings are great. But it is really "the convenience of having all repair bills paid for, and not having to take part in the auto business." So, from two or three cars to as many as 225, Cross-Canada Car Leasing deals with major pharmaceutical, steel, cosmetic, insurance, and manufacturing companies.

There were only three employees back in the early 1950s—the manager, one salesman, and a receptionist. But within a half-year the fledgling firm had close to 100 customers, and a great tradition had begun. Indeed, Cross-Canada has had growth every year since—and today has close to 50 people on staff.

Perhaps it is because Cross-Canada does not feature any one manufacturer's vehicles. "And by not being part of any dealership," says Gow, "we can provide everything from a basic compact to the most luxurious foreign import." Yes, they lease a number of Porsches.

It comes down to "controlling the customers' expenses, so they are all predetermined. This way, a business knows in advance what the automobiles will cost over the next two to three years," says chairman Robertson. "For more than 35 years we have paid for everything but gas."

Many accounts have been with Cross-Canada for more than 20 years. It is not by chance then that Cross-Canada Car Leasing Ltd. is now the largest company in full-maintenance leasing in all of Canada.

That is why the excellent firm has had nothing but success.

The oldest leasing company in Canada, Cross-Canada Car Leasing Ltd., has associated dealers and service centres from Victoria, British Columbia, to Gander, Newfoundland. The three main branches are located in (from left) St. Laurent, Quebec, and Scarborough and Mississauga, Ontario.

HENLEY CHEMICALS LTD.

Henley Chemicals moved to its new building in December 1984.

"We need chemicals in society," says David Mackenzie, president of Henley Chemicals Ltd. of Scarborough, one of the top dozen distribution agencies in Canada. "We can't live without them."

And it is clear that hundreds of Canadian companies have come to depend upon Henley since it opened its doors in 1979. It already had existing sales just exceeding one million dollars back then, since two West German companies had previously been selling directly into Canada. But when C.H. Boehringer from Ingelheim and Wacker-Chemie from Munich decided that they needed a presence in this country to distribute and sell their many fine chemical products, Henley Chemicals Ltd. was born.

The number of employees at the time of the firm's creation was only three, including a secretary; today it is more than 20. Fourteen staff members are located at the main office in Scarborough, the rest in Montreal, Edmonton, and Vancouver, to assist in distribution. But it is not only employees that are multiplying: The original sales back in its first year have increased almost exponentially since then, with sales of close to $20 million expected in 1987. That is a lot of chemicals.

There are two divisions to Henley Chemicals: Industrial, selling chemicals used in mining, coatings, paints, and sil-

icones, to give but a few examples, and Fine Chemicals, such as the ones used in detergents, pharmaceuticals, and personal care products such as hair conditioners and softeners.

The fine chemicals are widely accepted, but it is those industrial ones that David Mackenzie wants to emphasize in terms of safety. "We are very,

very cautious of what we store here, and we decided not to store any highly toxic chemicals in our 20,000-square-foot warehouse in Scarborough. We send the chemicals directly from the suppliers to the industries requiring them."

Not surprisingly, Henley chose to be based in Scarborough "due to the proximity to the main highway system, and we found the area clean, and serviced well. Most of our employees are from here, so we'll probably expand in the Scarborough area as well." And there is more than that: For although Henley does not manufacture anything on this side of the Atlantic yet, it is actually looking forward to manufacturing in Scarborough, a natural extension of the company's rapid growth.

What is also attractive about Henley is that it is not merely a branch plant of its two European parents. "All profits have been left in Canada, to build capital and allow expansion," says a pleased president Mackenzie.

In other words, while all of us need chemicals, Henley Chemicals Ltd. is thriving from them.

Chemical deliveries are made daily to customers throughout the area.

VOLKSWAGEN CANADA INC.

In the world of business, there is growth, and then there is phenomenal growth. In the case of Volkswagen Canada Inc., which sells and services some of the finest quality cars in the country, the growth has been astounding.

In 1952 the Canadian company was formed in Toronto with a staff of nine. That first year 94 Volkswagen cars were sold in this country. Just three years later the head office moved to Scarborough.

By 1984 the company had already started building component parts in a major, $44-million plant in Barrie, just north of the city. Nearly 5,000 employees worked for the Volkswagen organization across Canada, and sold approximately 40,000 Porsches, Audis, and Volkswagens per annum.

Today not only is Volkswagen Canada's national headquarters located in Scarborough, but also the Central Zone office. The head office, which employs more than 700 people, serves a national network of some 200 dealers and service centres, and has invested more than $80 million in facilities across Canada since the early 1950s.

The zone offices are strategically placed across Canada, with the Western Zone in Burnaby, British Columbia; the Quebec Zone in Pointe Claire, Quebec; and the Atlantic Zone in

Halifax, Nova Scotia. The Scarborough-based Central Zone services 80 dealers in Ontario, Manitoba, and Saskatchewan.

There are also three depots, with a total of some $84 million in parts inventory, and another $55 million-plus in dealer stock. Volkswagen Canada Re-

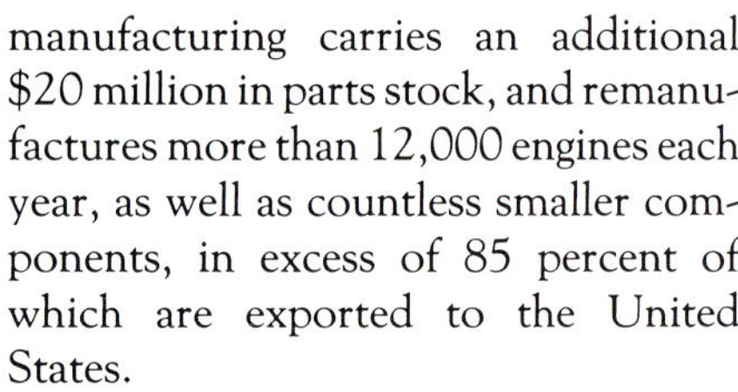

Volkswagen Canada's head office building in Scarborough.

Since 1984 Volkswagen Canada Inc. has been building component parts in this $44-million plant in Barrie.

manufacturing carries an additional $20 million in parts stock, and remanufactures more than 12,000 engines each year, as well as countless smaller components, in excess of 85 percent of which are exported to the United States.

Volkswagen Canada has certainly been successful during its 35 years in this country. The firm's continuing policy of encouraging the purchase of original equipment and aftermarket supply from Canadian manufacturers also considerably benefits the economy. More than $150 million worth of parts and accessories were purchased from Canadian companies in 1987 alone.

The wide model range of Volkswagens, Audis, and Porsches has meant good business for this country, and the corporate head office of Volkswagen Canada Inc. has meant good business for Scarborough, where the majority of the employees also live.

BICK'S PICKLES

In its pamphlet on the glory of its pickles and other superb products, Bick's writes ecstatically about the ancient heritage of that funny-sounding but delicious food: "The man who gave his name to the Americas, Amerigo Vespucci, was a pickle dealer before he became a famous navigator. And what of Cleopatra's passion for pickles? And the pickle love of Good Queen Bess of England?"

Well, pickles have their own impressive history within the boundaries of Scarborough, Ontario, as well. For it was way back in 1939 that Walter Bick and his family left their native Holland and settled at Knollview Farm, in what was then a farming community suburb of Toronto.

It was the Bick family that instituted its unique Fresh Pack processing in Canada in the early 1950s: They were the first picklemasters who packed their cucumbers fresh from the field, within 24 hours of harvesting.

That, and an inspired secret mix of spices, have truly made the difference. Today Bick's is the largest pickle processor in Canada, and its pickle plant near St. Catharines, Ontario, is the largest in all of North America—and possibly the world.

Every year Bick's buys in excess of one million bushels of cucumbers, and produces 3 million-plus cases of cucumber-based products. Then there are the beets, cabbage, cauliflower, corn, celery, olives, onions, peppers, pimentoes, tomatoes, and other ingredients of the firm's superior relishes.

For two decades now Bick's has been part of Robin Hood Multifoods Inc. of Canada, which includes Robin Hood flours, Old Mill oats, Coorsh smoked meats, desserts and salads, as well as many flours and yeasts for industry. And, in turn, Robin Hood is part of International Multifoods of Minneapolis.

But those are the parent companies. Bick's Pickles continues to provide consistent quality in its many products. "Making pickles is an art, not a science," insists a spokesman, and a tour of the firm's extraordinary plant proves the point.

Bick's support of many local soccer and baseball teams only underlines its closeness to the community where it began, and continues to thrive. It is also a large employer of students each summer, hiring nearly 100 at its main packing plant in Scarborough, and hundreds more down in Dunnville, Ontario, to pack the cucumbers.

"Most of our employees have been with us for many years," says Bick's Pickles' marketing manager. "There is a real commitment and loyalty to the products we put out for our consumers. And we pride ourselves on high-quality product, consistently delivered."

GOLDEN MILE MOTORS LTD./
SCARBOROUGH TOYOTA/NISSAN

There are countless successful entrepreneurs in the very exciting City of Scarborough. Bryan Rowntree, president of Golden Mile Motors Ltd./Scarborough Toyota Ltd., and much more, is an entrepreneur who is out to change the very nature and quality of his business.

Back in 1963 Rowntree joined the important General Motors dealership on the famous Golden Mile of Business, which had been at Pharmacy and Eglinton since the early 1950s. By 1974 he had managed to purchase the booming business from the Seitz family, and continued its excellent sales, "always in the 2,000-new-unit range."

Over the years Rowntree has gone from strength to strength. He created Scarborough Nissan in 1970, and went on to purchase Scarborough Toyota in 1980. As of today Bryan Rowntree owns nine dealerships, including three others in the Toronto area, three in Montreal, and, of course, the three in Scarborough.

It is all extraordinarily impressive—from his winning the *National Time Quality Dealer Award* in 1968, pre-

Golden Mile Motors Limited, 1897 Eglinton Avenue East.

just that. He set up a management company with the only full-time training for the auto industry in all of Canada; it requires four full-time instructors. The school has existed since the mid-1980s, teaching many hundreds of graduates about sales, business management, and service. Called Success Training and Management, it has "trained people literally from Nanaimo, British Columbia, to

Left: Scarborough Toyota Limited, 2000 Eglinton Avenue East.

Below: Scarborough Nissan, 1941 Eglinton Avenue East.

sented by the famous news magazine for all-around performance, to his sponsoring dozens of Scarborough's children's sporting teams. And with more than 600 employees at his nine dealerships (almost half of those at his three Scarborough locations), many of the employees have played on those earlier teams.

But that has never been enough for him. As he puts it, "We believe in continuous training programs. I spend nearly a half-million dollars a year in training people to be better and do better in this business."

And Rowntree has done more than

St. John's, Newfoundland."

In addition Rowntree sustains at least nine ongoing scholarships at Georgian College in Barrie, one hour north of Toronto, and is working with that institution for future development of his program for the benefit of the students.

"We are a progressive group," says Rowntree, "striving to make the auto industry a career and a profession for those who work in it. And when the young people graduate from Georgian College, they will be professionals."

And so, for more than one-third of a century, Golden Mile Motors Ltd. "has served the motoring needs of the Scarborough public." And, along with Rowntree's other impressive dealerships, "We've grown with Scarborough."

The firm is teaching a new generation to help the people and the city grow and succeed even more.

TOYOTA CANADA INC.

The expressions come fast and furious: "Toyota Quality." "The Toyota Family." "The Three Cs" (Communication/Co-operation/Consideration). "The Two Ps" (Professionalism/Productivity). "Good Thinking—Good Products." "Toyota . . . We Care."

Yet they work as well as the cars, and the men and women who make them. Take the last one for a moment. For the past number of years Toyota Canada Inc. has undertaken dozens of customer surveys, and then informed each of its 200-plus dealers across the country with hard evidence about problems at their respective stores, and how to deal with them.

Toyota certainly knows how to deal with the public, and has clearly sold them on what a superior product it has. Back in 1965, when the company's first cars were imported into Canada, a mere 755 cars were sold. In 1987 Toyota Canada had more than 5 percent of this country's market, and held the position of number one in import sales of cars and trucks, with a total of 83,065 sold. And Toyota's Forklift Division is number one in Canada, with more than 1,434 sales in 1987.

From Toyota Canada's president, Susumu Yanagisawa, and senior vice-president, Hector Dupuis, through its more than 300 employees in the Scarborough head office (and the additional 3,500-plus dealer personnel in every province), that concept of the Toyota Family is obviously a very real one, since it has made such names as Corolla, Celica, Cressida, Supra, Tercel, and Camry into household words in Canada.

Toyota was initially Canadian Motor Industries Ltd., out on the Eglinton Golden Mile, but by 1968 had broken ground on its 20.5 acres, 70,000 square feet of office space and 200,000 square feet of warehouse space on Bellamy Road North, near the Town Centre.

Since then the remarkable company has gone from strength to strength. An aluminum alloy wheel plant in Delta, British Columbia, followed in 1985, which is already undergoing a $26-million expansion; a new zone office in Calgary in 1986; another new zone office in Dartmouth, Nova Scotia, in 1987; and a $400-million plant in Cambridge, Ontario, will be turning out 50,000 Corollas in 1988 and beyond.

The investment in Canada has been astonishing: some $360 million in land, buildings, and equipment. More than $10.3 million in parts were sold in Montreal, Vancouver, and Toronto in May 1988 alone.

"Toyota will be the best," says a spokesman flatly. "It's a leader in electronics, such as computer-controlled engine, transmission, and air conditioning, all previously exotic features found only on the most expensive cars. We are the most advanced in robotics. It all fits together."

And with record months every month since March 1987, Toyota Canada Inc. has a lot to fit, celebrate, and maintain.

The Toyota Canada Inc. head office on Bellamy Road North in Scarborough.

MIDAS CANADA INCORPORATED

Millions of Canadians know of the witty and delightful commercials of Midas Mufflers, from their "Top Guns" to John "Moose" Quade declaiming, "On your feet, stringbean, ah'm talkin' to you!"

What they may not know is the phenomenal success of the company, its solid and deep presence in Scarborough, and the way it sets the industry standard in the auto aftermarket.

"We were the first to offer a lifetime guarantee on mufflers," says Roger Appleton, vice-president/sales and marketing, "the first to diversify into brake specialty service. And we're number one in market share, with around one million cars serviced each year." Adds Bob Bruce, manager of advertising and public relations, "We've got the most outlets—more than 200, as of the fall of 1987—and we service the most vehicles in our industry segment."

One should note that there was but a single shop in Scarborough in 1960; there are more than seven at the time of this writing. And the organization's 200-plus stores should number 275 by the end of 1992. Which is, in fact, a lot of mufflers, exhaust systems, shock ab-

A typical Midas outlet of the 1980s.

sorbers, brakes, and front-end services.

Midas began a half-century ago as the International Parts Corporation, which manufactured exhaust components. Then, in 1955, with its first shop, it pioneered the concept that would lead to its amazing growth: the franchising of retail shops specializing in auto exhaust system services.

Since coming to Canada in 1960—and the building of its handsome head office in Scarborough in 1976—the concept has taken off.

Midas came to Canada in 1960 and occupied the Scarborough head office and warehouse in 1976. The warehouse (left) encompasses 200,000 square feet.

There are more than 1,000 installers and managers in the firm's many shops, found in every province, and another 350 employees in Scarborough consist of office staff, warehouse, and manufacturing workers. The warehouse is a full 200,000 square feet in size, and the manufacturing plant, near Warden and Eglinton, has another 100,000 square feet.

Under the leadership of David Strolle, vice-president and general manager, Midas Canada continues to flourish, with sales in excess of $100 million in 1987. And, says Bob Bruce, "We've reinvested a lot of our profits into our Scarborough plant over the past number of years." Roughly $3 million, in fact, putting in an automated muffler line, and computerized pipe bending—and the vast majority of its employees are Scarborough residents.

There is the company's longstanding relationship with Big Brothers, and the nine years of sponsoring a soap box event. The Canadian Hearing Society and Muscular Dystrophy research also receive Midas' largesse.

But ultimately it is the reliable service, the convenient stores, the six warehouses (from Moncton to Vancouver), and the quality product that makes Midas Canada Incorporated truly the top gun in Canada.

MARVIN STARR PONTIAC BUICK INC.

Back in the spring of 1957, just exceeding three decades ago, a young salesman for a Buick dealer in Toronto asked his sales manager if he "could earn $6,000 a year."

"If you work hard," was the man's reply to Marvin Starr.

Marvin Starr and his close to 150 employees at Marvin Starr Pontiac Buick Inc. (up from a staff of 11 when he opened in Scarborough in 1968) have worked very hard.

There was a mild recession on when the rising Starr came east. He had already been a sales manager and had started Star Mercury in 1966. So when General Motors came to him and asked him to set up his Pontiac Buick dealership, he jumped at the chance. "You have to work good and hard in this business, and the timing was good," he says.

But there was still a great deal to do. There were merely five empty lots joined together when Starr set up shop on Eglinton Avenue East, near Markham Road. He designed and built his store "with a layout that was very different than what GM wanted." But, he adds, "I did it, and it worked."

The new dealership started out "like a house on fire," to quote the man with his name on the front of the building. His plan was to sell 1,450 cars in his first year; he ended up delivering 1,850. And another 1,200 used cars were sold as well. Marvin Starr Pontiac Buick Inc. sold 2,498 new cars and 750 used ones in 1987, in addition to running a "very large lease fleet."

Over the years the name Marvin Starr Pontiac Buick has been enscribed on the backs of hundreds of Scarborough children on baseball teams, hockey teams, and soccer teams, and the business happily supports Scarborough Centenary, as well as other major metropolitan hospitals.

And all the work—and good works—have paid off. Marvin Starr now runs the largest Pontiac Buick dealership in Scarborough, and is one of the top retail volume dealers of the nearly 1,000 General Motors dealers across Canada.

There are seven acres now, "we just bought another one," and the service centre was expanded in 1981. It is a drive-through now, and there is an indoor used car showroom. Every year the company keeps upgrading its equipment, with the latest computerized systems for car maintenance obtained at the cost of many hundreds of thousands of dollars.

Marvin Starr prides himself on his excellent reputation for service and adds, "GM is a good product, and getting better all the time."

Oh, yes, Marvin Starr earned $9,000 in his first six months as a salesman back in 1957, doing far better than he had even hoped. He must have worked harder.

The constantly expanding Marvin Starr Pontiac Buick Inc. dealership is located on seven acres on Eglinton Avenue East near Markham Road. Equipped with a drive-through service centre, there is also an indoor used-car showroom and the latest in computerized systems for car maintenance.

MINOLTA BUSINESS EQUIPMENT (CANADA) LTD.

Sometimes numbers tell quite a bit about a company and its success. In December 1975 Minolta Business Equipment (Canada) Ltd. opened its doors in a 1,500-square-foot office in Scarborough, with three employees and no previous clientele. In its first fiscal year it sold less than $200,000 in copiers. As of 1987, less than a dozen years later, there were 33 employees in a new, 40,000-square-foot Scarborough head office (with a subsidiary in Alberta that has another 100 employees). And the firm's sales are topping $25 million, with 30 percent more growth expected by the end of 1988.

Sometimes a name can mean a lot, too. Minolta has been providing leadership in technology for a half-century. From its first single-lens reflex camera in 1958, to production of its first copier the following year, to the world's first enlargement copier in 1980, to the world's first automatic zoom copier in 1983, Minolta has been a highly respected name in industry, science, medicine, and agriculture, as well as cameras and copiers, since 1928.

The man who was chosen by Minolta to start its business equipment venture in Canada is also a significant factor. Costos Angelakis is the son of Greek immigrants to Canada, born and raised in Montreal, but working in Toronto since 1972. Angelakis had been working for Litton Business Systems of Canada distributing Royal Typewriters, but when the company gave up

Minolta's 40,000-square-foot national head office and main warehouse on Finchdene Square in Scarborough.

its Canadian franchise, he was asked to liquidate it. He was approached by Minolta, "just as the copier business was starting to boom."

It was an inspired choice, for Angelakis and for his bosses in New Jersey (Minolta Corporation) and Japan (Minolta Camera Co. Ltd.). Of course, the success was certainly helped by the excellence of the product. "We have very good machines. And we're measured in the industry by the good copies we make." The Buyers Laboratory Inc. report in the January 1987 issue of *Copier Review* labelled the Minolta EP 470Z Best Desktop Copier. To quote the review, it was "one of the few units

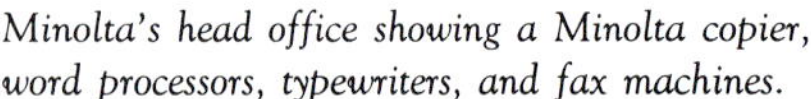

Minolta's head office showing a Minolta copier, word processors, typewriters, and fax machines.

among those tested by BLI that was a pleasure to evaluate . . . Throughout testing, this desktop model performed smoothly and displayed consistently excellent copy quality, excellent reliability, and minimal jamming. Since the test unit rarely required service, it breezed through a 90,000-copy test." One can understand why Minolta is now in the top five in the very crowded copier market in Canada, holding some 10 percent of the business.

Minolta Business Equipment (Canada) Ltd. puts "a lot of concentration on service," says Angelakis, with a half-dozen national technicians, and continual training nearly every month of the year. "We stand behind our product," he emphasizes, "and get involved directly with the dealer and the customer."

The incentive program must also help—all successful dealers go on annual trips to such locations as Honolulu, Paris, Amsterdam, Munich, Ireland, and Monte Carlo, where Minolta of Canada introduces the latest extraordinary advance in copiers.

But, as with all successful businesses, it comes down to quality, dependability, and service. With Costos Angelakis leading the way, and vice-president Yvon St. Yves "in charge of all operation," Minolta Business Equipment (Canada) Ltd. has a bright future.

PATRONS

The following individuals, companies, and organizations have made a valuable commitment to the quality of this publication. Windsor Publications and The Scarborough Chamber of Commerce gratefully acknowledge their participation in *Scarborough: An Economic Celebration*.

Beverley Hills Home Improvements*
Bick's Pickles*
Centenary Hospital*
Centennial College*
The City of Scarborough*
Clarkson Gordon*
Command Records Services Limited*
Commercial Union Life Assurance Company of Canada*
Cross-Canada Car Leasing Ltd.*
East Scarborough Boys' and Girls' Club*
Foster Pontiac Buick Ltd.*
General Motors of Canada Limited*
Golden Mile Motors Ltd./Scarborough Toyota/Nissan*
The Guild Inn*
Henley Chemicals Ltd.*
Herity Group of Companies*
Hogan Chevrolet-Oldsmobile Ltd.*
Honda Canada Inc.*
Kaiser Aluminum and Chemical of Canada Limited*
Lebovic Enterprises Limited*
Med-Chem Laboratories Limited*
Midas Canada Incorporated*
Minolta Business Equipment (Canada) Ltd.*
Monarch Investments Limited*
Nienkamper*
Phillips Cables Limited*
The Prudential Insurance Company of America*
The Public Utilities Commission of the City of Scarborough*
Rex Pak Ltd.*
Royal LePage Real Estate Services Ltd.*
Runnymede Development Corporation Limited*
Scarborough Grace General Hospital*
ScotiaMcCleod*
Shorewood Packaging Corporation of Canada Limited*
SKF Canada Limited*
Marvin Starr Pontiac Buick Inc.*
Toyota Canada Inc.*
Tridel*
Trilea Centres Inc.*
Volkswagen Canada Inc.*
Welcome Wagon Ltd.*
Williams Brothers Corporation*

*Partners in Progress of *Scarborough: An Economic Celebration*. The histories of these companies and organizations appear in Part Two, beginning on page 109.

AFTERWORD

The Scarborough Chamber of Commerce

The headline of the editorial in the *Scarborough Mirror*, September 13, 1986, announced in very clear terms: "Business Association Becomes Dynamic, New Chamber of Commerce." It was a formal, serious step for an organization that had, in the words of the *Mirror*, grown "incredibly" since its founding a half-dozen years before.

As the Scarborough Business Association, its membership had grown to some 700 members; with the news of its change of name and focus, its numbers quickly grew to well over 800.

By the time of this writing—the summer of 1988—the Scarborough Chamber of Commerce had increased by more than half, to fully 1,300 members, and had 16 committees working on issues of significant community interest. A variety of Chamber-sponsored activities were creating even more opportunities for involvement on the part of its membership—such as "hands on" workshops that dealt with manufacturing, energy conservation, marketing, and networking. Surveys were also being taken among this important, constantly growing cross-section of the business community of the city of Scarborough: What did they think about the Free Trade question? About Sunday openings? About the activities of the Chamber of Commerce?

The activities of the Chamber bespeak an intelligent, creative approach to progress in Scarborough:

*During an eight-week period in the spring of 1988, the Entrepreneurial Development Committee of the SCC approved 26 loans of approximately $3,000 each to Scarborough youth, to help them set up and operate their own small businesses during the summer.

*The Chamber has been participating in COIN. (Computerized Ontario Investment Network), an innovative computer system which puts investors with capital in touch with businesses. Amounts ranging from $5,000 up to $500,000 can be offered or sought through COIN.

*A vital programme of energy conservation is being carried out by the Chamber in co-operation with the province's Ministry of Energy, to help improve energy efficiency of buildings throughout Scarborough.

*A liaison between the business and education communities has been established through the creation of an Industry-Education Council.

There is much more going on thanks to the Chamber's many committees, whose functions range from welcoming new members and guests, to a major push to increase tourism to Scarborough, to the production of the handsome book you presently hold in your hands.

In a nutshell, the Scarborough Chamber of Commerce, still in its first few years of life, has already fulfilled the hopeful prediction of that 1986 editorial which had welcomed its creation: "With an optimistic outlook and a positive sense of direction, the Scarborough Chamber of Commerce could be a strong force to reckon with—and an incredibly successful support system for Scarborough's business community."

The provincial, Canadian, and city flags stand outside the Civic Centre. Photo by Glen Jones

INDEX

Italicized numbers indicate illustrations